Mothman

Other Cosimo Books by Loren Coleman

Mothman and Other Curious Encounters

Loren Coleman Presents
(with new Introductions by Loren Coleman)

Abominable Snowmen: Legend Come to Life by Ivan T. Sanderson
Curiosities of Natural History, Vols. 1–4 by Francis T. Buckland
Curious Creatures in Zoology by John Ashton
Dragons and Dragon Lore by Ernest Ingersoll
Gleanings from the Natural History of the Ancients by Morgan George Watkins
Mythical Monsters by Charles Gould
Natural History Lore and Legend by Frederick Edward Hulme
Oddities: A Book of Unexplained Facts by Rupert T. Gould
Sea Fables Explained by Henry Lee
Sea Monsters Unmasked by Henry Lee
The Book of Werewolves by Sabine Baring-Gould
The Dragon, Image, and Demon by Hampden C. DuBose
The Dragon in China and Japan by Marinus Willem De Visser
The Great Sea Serpent by Antoon Cornelis Oudemans
The Romance of The Unicorn by Robert Brown
Natural History by Philip Henry Gosse
The Werewolf by Montague Summers
Thunderbirds: America's Living Legends of Giant Birds by Mark A. Hall

MOTHMAN
Evil Incarnate

The Unauthorized Companion to
The Mothman Prophecies

Loren Coleman

Cosimo Books
New York, New York

Cosimo aims to publish books that inspire, inform, and engage readers worldwide. We use innovative print-on-demand technology that enables books to be printed based on specific customer needs. This approach eliminates an artificial scarcity of publications and allows us to distribute books in the most efficient and environmentally sustainable manner. Cosimo also works with printers and paper manufacturers who practice and encourage sustainable forest management, using paper that has been certified by the FSC, SFI, and PEFC whenever possible.

Ordering Information:
Cosimo publications are available at online bookstores. They may also be purchased for educational, business, or promotional use:

Bulk orders: Special discounts are available on bulk orders for reading groups, organizations, businesses, and others.

Custom-label orders: We offer selected books with your customized cover or logo of choice.

For more information, contact us at www.cosimobooks.com.

Contents

To Jenny

Introduction

You do know about Mothman, don't you? This book assumes a basic familiarity with the large mysterious flying creature seen in Point Pleasant, West Virginia, in 1966–1967—a remarkable series of events that culminated with the collapse of the Silver Bridge, which killed 46 people. You have probably read the classic work on the subject by John Keel, *The Mothman Prophecies*, and if not, you certainly should do so. I like to view that book as a cryptozoological version of Truman Capote's *In Cold Blood*.

Or maybe you saw the movie of the same name, which was directed by Mark Pellington in 2002, although as with most Hollywood productions, truth was not exactly its primary concern.

Or maybe you read my book on the subject, *Mothman and Other Curious Encounters*, which was released when the movie appeared; that book provided a context for sightings of Mothman and its precursors.

There have also been a few documentaries on the subject, one of the best being the recently released Small Town Monsters production, *The Mothman of Point Pleasant*, directed by Seth Breedlove.

So, assuming you do know about Mothman, you probably can't help but wonder: is there some deep evil at the bottom of all this?

I will explore that subject in this book and bring the Mothman story up to date. We'll begin with a rundown of the most recent sightings of the creature, profile the writer who brought the story to life, fill in details of the Hollywood movie, look into the deaths that followed it, explain what effect these events have had on that small West Virginia town, and comment on the documentaries that have attempted to come to grips with the Mothman mystery. And, of course, we'll look in detail at the book that put the creature out in the ether, ready to invade your nightmares.

CHAPTER 1

Breaking News—Chicago 2017: Madness, Mayhem and Mothman

When a reporter in the mainstream media pays atten-tion to what are normally fringe reports of strange flying creatures, you can be sure that something *really* is going on. Such was the case on July 29, 2017, when the *Chicago Tribune* ran a Ted Slowik column entitled "Chicago's 'Mothman' stories are good paranormal entertainment."

It was written with that slight edge of ridicule and humor that reporters often use to give themselves an out, just in case anyone might think they are taking the accounts too seriously. Slowik wrote: "When I heard about recent alleged sightings of 'Mothman' in Chicago, I reacted with a healthy dose of skepticism."

But deep down, the *Chicago Tribune* column acknowledged the encounters were something to be confronted openly, with more than a grain of salt. The eyewitness reports seemed to be straightforward accounts that, as a whole, could indicate some-thing was happening.

In fact, the 2017 Mothman sightings in Chicago represent the biggest concentration of Mothman sighting since the events in West Virginia 50 years ago. Is it a coincidence that Chicago is seeing its highest murder rate in decades?

The sightings in the Chicago area all began in the spring of 2017. The primary researcher was Lou Strickler of Hanover, Pennsylvania, who heads the *Phantoms and Monsters* website (phantomsandmonsters.com). He has documented scores of experiences, accounts, and sightings in the Chicago area beginning in March and continuing beyond August 2017. Everything from a seven-foot-tall, red-eyed bat to "black shapes" have been reported as "Mothman."

Here is a brief overview of some of the cases from the Chicago area.

March 2017

One of the earliest sightings, as often happens, was revealed later, but for the sake of this chronology, I will mention it first.

On March 22, 2017, a local Chicago truck driver named Billy Bantz was making a delivery when he noticed something weird in the sky. "It looked like a flying Batmobile," he reported to Strickler. "I was sitting in my semi–trailer at around noon. I saw this object coming from Route 55 and Cicero. I saw it gliding, and, not too fast. No sound. I saw that it was not a drone, and the size of a large car. It climbed higher and turned twice…I can tell you that it glided just like a bird. It went almost straight up and I lost it in the clouds."

Bantz says that this incident has affected his life. "The more I speak of this," he said, "the worse my luck becomes. My mom died three weeks ago. I am not sure what to think at this point."

So, the underlying evil of this "Mothman" revealed itself almost immediately.

April 2017

The first encounter of record in the media was on April 7, 2017. It came from an unnamed witness who saw a seven-foot-tall, manlike bird in Oz Park, in the North Side-Lincoln Park neighborhood of Chicago, Illinois. The observer claimed to be jogging with a dog in the park at night, when his pet became spooked by something, and the birds in the park suddenly went silent.

The description of the winged creature is vaguely similar to the infamous Mothman of Point Pleasant: "It was about 7 feet tall ... it looked like a giant half-man, half-bird kind of thing ... These wings looked almost bat-like and were at least 10 feet across from tip to tip ... It rose into the air like a bullet and I heard it screech once more before losing it from my view as it rose above the trees and possibly the buildings."

This report sparked a reaction, encouraging many witnesses to come forward and report their own stories of a "flying humanoid" in the Chicago area.

Next came reports from boaters on Lake Michigan, who saw a large flying creature circling overhead between 10:00 pm on April 15, 2017, and 2:00 am on the morning of April 16, 2017. One of the witnesses gave this description: "We were about two miles out on the lake, just off of Montrose at about 10 pm. We were enjoying ourselves when I happen to look up and saw what looked like a giant bat, and not like a [flying] fox bat. This bat was as tall as my husband, who is 6-foot, 4-inches, or even bigger. This bat circled the boat three times in complete silence before heading off towards Montrose. It quickly blended into the night sky and was gone in seconds."

The eyewitness appears to be referring to "flying foxes" (of the genus *Pteropus*, belonging to the megabat suborder, Megachiroptera) that are familiar to Americans from nature shows on television. These flying foxes live in the tropics and subtropics of Asia (including the Indian subcontinent), Australia, East Africa, and a number of remote oceanic islands in both the Indian and Pacific Oceans. But there have been no reports of escaped flying foxes in the Midwest in recent years.

Later in the day on April 15, 2017, Chicago witnesses said they saw *la lechuza*, a barn owl aligned with Mexican folklore. They reported: "We walked over there and saw what looked like big owl. As we walked up on it, this owl stood up on two feet and looked right at us. We saw what looked like a huge Lechuza, except it was about six feet tall and really big. It had large glowing red eyes that were completely freaking everybody out."

Another account on April 15, 2017, took place near the Chicago International Produce Market. According to the witness in Strickler's report: "I looked up and saw the biggest freaking owl I have ever seen! I'm 6 foot, 2 inches, and I'm guessing this thing was at least a foot taller than me. It was completely black except for it having bright yellowish/reddish eyes like a cat. It stood there for a minute or two staring at everyone before shooting up into the sky and disappearing. It made everyone feel very uneasy and only took off after some guys threw some rocks at it. It had wings on it like an owl, only bigger and you could hear it flap those wings when it took off."

May 2017
Sightings of the "evil" entity continued throughout May 2017.

Along the Lakeview Avenue area, Chicago, on Saturday, May 27, 2017, a couple noticed something overhead like a giant bat, only larger and solid black with two glowing red eyes. It circled back and flew over the couple again before heading back toward the park. Strickler said that the couple waited for about one month before reporting their sighting.

June 2017
On June 3, 2017, a couple saw a winged weirdie in the Lincoln Park area around 10:00 pm local time. The couple, who wishes to remain anonymous, had just finished a late dinner and were out for a walk when they saw the strange being. After talking with them on the phone, Strickler described what they saw: "it was a 7–8 ft solid black humanoid with wide membrane wings that resembled those of a huge bat. The wingspan was at least 12 feet. The head was prominent, and thinner than a human head. The back end of the body tapered to a point. No legs were noticed, but could have been tucked up under the body. The figure was gliding quickly along the length of the street heading east, then suddenly ascended into the night sky. Neither heard any sound."

Both witnesses told Strickler that they felt a sense of foreboding and were still terrified almost an hour after the encounter.

The month of June had several sightings, but one of the more interesting ones happened on June 29, 2017, at approximately 11:15 pm, in the Auburn Gresham neighborhood in Chicago. A witness was walking home from getting some food at Wendy's with a small group of friends, when one of the friends pointed at a dark shape in a tree on the corner of West 81st and South Throop streets. The thing was big, although hard to make out at night. It then jumped out of the tree and flew onto the roof of an apartment building on the same block. When it flew, the witness got the chance to see that it was a tall dark creature with wide wings. A group of people had started to form on the corner with the witness and their friends. Some of the people flagged down a police car to point the thing out. It flew away soon thereafter.

July 2017
Three witnesses in a car traveling north on Lake Shore Drive, Chicago, Illinois, on Thursday, July 20, 2017, at 5:00 pm local time, noticed an animate object like a giant black flying bat emerging from under the overpass at East Grand Avenue. It flew swiftly upwards over the trees and in the direction of Lake Michigan.

Another encounter occurred across from the Harold Washington Library Center (400 S State Street) in downtown Chicago, a week later, at 8:45 pm on Thursday, July 27, 2017. The witness saw a large, bat-like creature perched atop a streetlight pole across the street from the Library. The creature stood about seven feet tall and was sitting motionless. The unidentifiable thing had a pair of glowing red eyes that appeared to be fixated on something across the street. It stood there for about six seconds. The observer noticed a flash from a group of kids on the sidewalk as someone was taking a picture of the beast. It then spread open a large pair of wings, flapped them a couple of times, and took off into the air. The girls from the group of kids screamed, and they all took off running. The witness saw it shoot up and over the library; it was gone in a matter of about two seconds. Shaken up by what he had seen, the witness spoke to his pastor about it at church on Saturday. The pastor recommended that he report the sighting to those investigating the incidents. No photographs have surfaced.

August 2017

Reports continued to come in at a rapid pace, often followed by sinister physical reactions. On August 9, 2017, at 9:20 pm, an encounter took place at 1400 N. Lake Shore Drive and East Schiller Street. It involved a large winged creature that had the eyewitnesses feeling "a vibration that emanated from the being." One female eyewitness, identified only as "AG," stated that she literally "fell to her knees" after the incident, and that her husband had to assist her the rest of the way home. Afterwards, the witnesses reported being unable to sleep for more than an hour or two a night.

Another witness who saw a "big owl" circling the lake off Ohio Street Beach on August 10, at 7:30 pm, would not identify herself because she works for the City of Chicago government and did not want to jeopardize her job. But she did say, "I can tell you that these sightings have not gone unnoticed and have garnered much attention, but there are powers to [*sic*] be that do not want the increasing number of sightings to jeopardize the summer and potentially scare away tourists. But please know that these sightings have not gone unnoticed within City Hall."

Two days later on Sunday August 13, 2017 at Grant Park, at around 9:30 pm, after the Lollapalooza music festival, a couple noticed a large thing flying overhead. When they came across it in a park, the creature unfolded its wings and took off into the air. Both witnesses described the red-eyed, bat-like creature as approximately seven feet tall and completely black with a 10-foot wingspan. It had a pair of red eyes that glowed, claimed the observers. The creature then flapped its wings and was gone.

One of the latest notable sightings happened on the day of the solar eclipse. On Monday, August 21, 2017, at Burnham

Harbor, Chicago, Illinois, at about 1:15 pm, just before the solar eclipse, three friends heard squeaking and saw a large object flying overhead. This object looked like a large black bat, but with humanoid features, such as pronounced arms and legs. The creature was six or seven feet tall, with wings at least eight-feet wide. According to those who saw it, it was real flesh and blood and was "quite scary."

What's going on?
Lon Strickler received numerous reports on the rash of sightings in Chicago and tried to investigate every case. "Each witness," he said, "has had a feeling of dread and foreboding."

But Strickler was not alone in seeking an answer to this mystery. As reports continued to come in over the months, Vance Nesbitt and Jennifer Ann, hosts of *The Acrylic Ranch* podcast, went out on their own night investigations to try and obtain some footage of the monster. They experienced some odd battery drains on their equipment while in the area.

Milwaukee researchers Kimberly Poeppey and Allison Jornlin also conducted investigations in Illinois in the late summer of 2017. Poeppey, by bizarre coincidence, did find a vintage Mothman mug at a Goodwill store, a relatively rare find. They filmed turkey vultures, but did not have any sightings of the "Chicago Mothman."

It's not surprising that these Chicagoland creatures were referred to as "Mothman," as the comparisons with the old accounts from West Virginia in 1966–1967 are obvious. People took the handy label and thought no more about the various descriptions. But what becomes apparent from a deeper look at the accounts is how many different types of flying things were actually being reported. A few researchers argued some people were probably seeing a large owl. Other witnesses described the "creatures" as more bat-like. Actual hominoid flying beasts are described infrequently. Kites seemed to be involved too. And one investigator for MUFON thought that at least some of the reports were a hoax, a student project of some kind, or perhaps performance art. In any case, a bit of mass hysteria certainly seemed to be involved, as well.

Although testimony concerning the appearances varies, one recurring theme seems to be consistent. The witnesses were often overcome with a feeling of dire terror, and a sense that tragedy would result in the wake of any sighting. The Banshee-like folkloric nature of the Mothman had resurfaced and went hand-in-hand with most of the Illinois incidents, even if no evidence of a major tragedy has resulted from the sightings. At least not so far.

The sightings continue.

CHAPTER 2

The Writer:
Fascinating, Fortean, and Frustrating

John Keel is best known for his seminal work, *The Mothman Prophecies*. But there is much more to John Keel than that. He was born Alva John Kiehle in upstate New York on March 25, 1930. He began writing at a young age. Keel's first story was published in a magician's magazine at the age of 12. He would go on to become a scriptwriter for radio and television, and a stringer for newspapers. He later moved to Greenwich Village in New York City and wrote for various men's and specialty magazines.

Keel's first published book was *Jadoo* in 1957 (republished after his death by Anomalist Books), which was serialized in a men's adventure magazine. This work is his account of his journey of discovery to what in the 1950s was known as the Orient to investigate the alleged activities of fakirs and holy men who perform the Indian rope trick and who survive being buried alive. In *Jadoo*, Keel also told of tracking a Yeti, an Abominable Snowman, in the jungles of Asia.

Then came his 1966 novel *The Fickle Finger of Fate*, Keel's humorous look at life's unplanned twists. It is a rare book, and few realize that Keel wrote it.

John Keel was an early admirer of Charles Fort (1874–1932). Then, after being influenced by zoologist Ivan T. Sanderson and ufologist Aimé Michel in early 1966, Keel began a full-time investigation of monsters, UFOs, and paranormal phenomena. While still writing for the mainstream, he started authoring articles for England's *Flying Saucer Review* (*FSR*) and a long series of columns for *Saga* magazine, including one 1967 article entitled "UFO Agents of Terror," which referred to the Men in Black. He also wrote one of the first articles on Mothman in *FSR*, during this same time period.

Over a four-year stretch in the 1960s, Keel interviewed thousands of people in over 20 U.S. states, especially in the Ohio River Valley of the United States. He claimed to have read more than 2,000 books in the course of his investigation, in addition to thousands of magazines, newsletters, and newspapers. Keel also subscribed to several newspaper-clipping services, which often generated up to 150 clippings for a single day during the 1966 and 1967 UFO "wave."

Like other contemporary 1960s researchers such as J. Allen Hynek and Jacques Vallée, Keel was initially hopeful that he could somehow validate the prevailing nuts-and-bolts, extraterrestrial visitation hypothesis for UFOs. However, a year into his investigations, Keel realized that the extraterrestrial hypothesis was untenable and did not provide all the answers. Keel's insights also included his view of cryptozoology.

I came to know Keel after being introduced to him through mutual friends Brad Steiger and Ivan Sanderson. I worked closely with Keel on contributing as yet-unpublished material of mine for his book *Strange Creatures from Time and Space* (1970), which would influence two books I wrote with Jerome Clark: *The Unidentified* (1975) and *Creatures from the Outer Edge* (1978).

John Keel was both controversial and popular. He was one of the most widely read and influential Fortean authors of the late 20th century. Although his thoughts about Fortean phenomena evolved during the 1960s, Keel remained one of Ufology's most original and controversial researchers.

It was Keel's second non-fiction book, *UFOs: Operation Trojan Horse* (1970), which alerted the general public that many aspects of contemporary UFO reports, including humanoid encounters, often paralleled certain ancient folklore and religious encounters. Keel also argued that there is a direct relationship between UFOs and spirit phenomena. Keel told me often that he did not consider himself a "ufologist," but a "demonologist." Said Keel: "Ufology is just another name for demonology."

As Keel wrote in *UFOs: Operation Trojan Horse*, "I abandoned the extraterrestrial hypothesis in 1967 when my own field investigations disclosed an astonishing overlap between psychic phenomena and UFOs... The objects and apparitions do not necessarily originate on another planet and may not even exist as permanent constructions of matter. It is more likely that we see what we want to see and interpret such visions according to our contemporary beliefs."

Keel argued that a non-human or spiritual intelligence source has staged whole events over a long period of time in order to propagate and reinforce certain erroneous belief systems. Keel conjectured that ultimately all anomalies, such as fairies, 1897 mystery airships, 1930s phantom aeroplanes, mystery helicopters, poltergeists, balls of light, UFOs, and creatures like Bigfoot and Mothman are a cover for the real phenomenon.

It was during this time period that Keel maintained an enormous and active correspondence with other researchers around the world. For example, Keel introduced me to my now long-time friend Jerry Clark, via letters. These exchanges between Keel and his fellow writers and researchers, even as intellectual disagreements and different paths took many of us on varied journeys, cemented 50 years of solid friendships among a small group of dedicated Fortean writers.

In *Our Haunted Planet* (1971), Keel coined the term "ultraterrestrials" to describe the UFO occupants. He discussed the seldom-considered possibility that the alien "visitors" to Earth are not visitors at all, but an advanced Earth civilization, which may or may not be human. Keel took no position on the ultimate purpose of the phenomenon other than that the UFO intelligence seems to have a long-standing interest in interacting with the human race.

UFO historian Jerome Clark wrote in *The UFO Encyclopedia, Volume 1: UFOs in the 1980s* that Keel was "a radical theorist who believes that UFOs are 'ultraterrestrial' rather than extraterrestrial. By that he means they are shape-changing phenomena from another order of existence. These ultraterrestrials are basically hostile to, or at least contemptuous of, human beings and manipulate them in various ways, for example by staging 'miracles' which inspire unfounded religious beliefs. Ultraterrestrials and their minions may manifest as monsters, space people, ghosts and other paranormal entities."

After years of writing parts of the story in various articles and other books, in 1975, Keel published *The Mothman Prophecies*, an account of a "winged weirdie" reported in and around Point Pleasant, West Virginia, in 1966–1967. Keel had corresponded with Ivan T. Sanderson, quietly for months, trying to determine what kind of bird might be involved with the sightings.

Then in 2002 the movie based on the book was released. It was directed by Mark Pellington and starred Richard Gere, Debra Messing, Laura Linney, and Alan Bates. Just as the movie was being released, a rumor circulated that Keel had died. The story appeared on the internet on January 14, 2002. I quickly put the rumor to rest by calling Keel and confirming that he was, indeed, still alive. Keel quipped that everyone should be told, "his funeral is on Saturday and he will be wearing black." Keel noted that this had happened to him at least once before, back in 1967.

Keel used the movie to publish one last swipe at all of his old friends. Tor Books republished Keel's book with a new afterword by the author when the movie appeared. Keel used the opportunity to express his displeasure and thoughts, saying that people had "stolen" his ideas. Keel was getting crusty back in 2002.

Then in 2006, Keel suffered a heart attack. He admitted himself to New York City's Lenox Hill Hospital on Friday the 13th of October, and underwent successful heart surgery three days later. Keel then was moved from the hospital to a rehabilitation center on October 26, 2006.

Warren Allen Smith, a well-known gay activist and the author of *Who's Who in Hell* and other books, shared a room with Keel at the assisted care center. Smith later wrote me saying: "I was John Keel's roommate at the Greenwich Village Nursing Home, and he delighted in having an intellectual to talk to (although an Asimov friend and sci-fi academic). He had been there for weeks and was a pain to the staff, as they were to him. When it came time for him to be released, he fought to stay in, saying he'd not paid rent at his apartment, that it would need cleaning, his car in the garage likely had flat tires, he had only one tooth, and many other problems with no friends whatsoever that he could trust. When he did pack to leave, he was angry as hell (not Hell, I pointed out to him, which is a theistic term describing a non-existent place). How he survived from November 2008 to July 2009 is a mystery to me!"

Keel passed away on Friday, July 3, 2009, at Mount Sinai Hospital in New York City, after some months in that nursing home near his Upper West Side apartment in New York City, where he lived most of his life.

Correspondents who were with him at the end have provided some shockingly sad details of his lonely, unfortunate last days. One who wrote was Keel's niece, Nicole. It turns out that Nicole's mother, John's half-sister Cheryl, had been trying to reach John for weeks and said his cell phone number wasn't working. John's and Cheryl's mother was Irene Gibbs Kiley. The family had not been notified about John's passing until they saw my obituary. Of course, Nicole was upset because Keel's family had lost track of him, and this was the first they heard that John had died. They knew of the past "death rumors" and wanted to make certain this one was the truth. It was.

Eventually, Nicole's mother reached me and we talked for nearly half an hour. Cheryl Gaye is Keel's youngest sister, actually his half-sister. John, who was 79, and his siblings shared the same mother, but he had a different father than his younger brother (68) and sisters (66, 64). John's father was Harry Kiehle; he separated from Irene during the Great Depression and, for financial reasons, John Keel (the family name changed when he began to write extensively) never finished high school.

Cheryl was rather frantic because the family had not heard from John since New Year's Day 2009, and despite leaving messages on his cell phone, he never returned any calls. The family feared the phone was broken or disconnected. After 9/11, John, who was close to Cheryl, had driven his Toyota Echo all the way out to her place in Perry, New York, where he stayed for several days. At that time, Keel told his sister that he wanted to move out of New York, away from what he thought were the continued dangers of New York City. But Keel never could get himself in a financially stable or healthy enough position to leave his apartment. After a while, Keel refused to travel by air as well. (Keel was supposed to fly to Point Pleasant to appear in the Mothman documentary on 9/11. Forever after that, he was uncomfortable with flying.)

In his last years, Keel just didn't want to be bothered; he didn't want anyone to know his phone number or address, and certainly avoided media interviews as much as possible. Those who tried to help him were distrusted, and towards the end, Keel's signs of paranoia were overt and got in the way of him having relatively normal human interactions.

Keel has had an enormous effect on popular culture. His impact cannot be underestimated, especially in terms of his analysis of patterns. His work on the three "Ws"—"windows" (specific hotspots of combined phenomenal appearances), "waves" (cyclic appearances of the phenomena), and the "Wednesday phenomenon" (the theory that a disproportionate number of UFO events occur on that day of the week)—have been deeply influential. Keel was there first, looking for such patterns. Future academic studies will be needed to fully realize his reach among the subculture fascinated by the denizens of his ongoing intellectual playground.

John Keel was a frustrating friend to the end. Deep down, I will always think of John Keel as a good and decent person, with a wry sense of humor. I appreciated the old John, the fellow Fortean traveler, the citation-heavy correspondent, the friendly Mothman researcher, even though he cut off contact with many of us in his waning weeks. When his Mothman movie came out (for that's how we all thought of it), he knew I was working with the studio to take a bit of the burden for the promotions off his back. So when the movie studio asked me to do a new companion book on the Mothman, the ole gracious John came through generously with a blurb for *Mothman and Other Curious Encounters*. He wrote: "After a lifetime of research, Loren Coleman has produced the most complete overview of Mothman and its minions—the scariest family of monsters on Earth."

I want to thank Doug Skinner, Larry Sloman, and Anthony Matt, all in New York City, who helped John so much in his last years. Doug Skinner, who was with him at the end, posted this: "Fortunately, his last stay [in the hospital] wasn't long, and he was mostly cogent and ambulatory until a couple of days before he died. He was in a coma Friday [July 3rd], but I told him we'd done all we could for him, that we'd miss him, and that we'd keep reading his crazy books, and bid him good-bye."

Richard Hatem penned a touching tribute of Keel in his blog on July 7, 2009: "John enjoyed the resurgence of interest in Mothman—and his writings. The most gratifying part of it all being that a whole new generation of readers were introduced to his work. Whether any of his theories are ever proven or not, John Keel will—and should—have a long-lasting readership based solely on the fact that he was a tremendously entertaining writer."

CHAPTER 3

The Book:
Dedicated, Diabolical, and Detailed

The phenomenon known as Mothman today would likely not be as infamous, if not for the work of New York reporter John Keel. He was one of the major forces behind how UFO and paranormal phenomena are perceived in the modern world. People claim to have been abducted by aliens, controlled by them, even impregnated with human/alien cross-breeds—Keel took down stories like these back in the 1960s from frightened and confused folk he termed "silent contactees." (Contactees are persons who claim to have experienced interactions with extraterrestrials, historically reaching a peak during the 1940s and 1950s. Keel would extend this to include ultraterrestrials in the 1960s and 1970s.)

The concept that paranormal phenomena are all related somehow—"The Phenomenon" as some investigators call it—is an idea that had its seeds in the books of Charles Fort but became the central theme in the works of Keel.

Keel has written voluminously about "Window Areas," "flaps" of UFO and monster sightings, the "Name Game," synchronicities having to do with days of the month and specific areas on the map, and the "reflexive" nature of Fortean events. His ideas have been touched upon in almost every book on the unexplained published in the last 50 years. He is simultaneously the subtle influence behind, and the vociferous bad boy of, ufology and forteana.

Keel's book *The Mothman Prophecies* details his personal trip beyond the looking glass. But the book is not perfect; no book is actually. Keel was sometimes fooled by hoaxes, and his book contains numerous mistakes. That's a reality that every writer on the unexplained has had to confront. If only there was someone who cared enough to research the sources that busy writers and reporters have used in their work.

Enter Michael D. Winkle. Monsters in the movies, the comics, literature, mythology, folklore, and even (maybe) reality have always captivated him. By age 11, Winkle thought he knew all there was to know about ghosts, monsters, and bizarre creatures in general.

Then one night Winkle's father took him and his brother to the bowling alley. They were expected to entertain themselves while he bowled for the Warren Petroleum Company league. Winkle slipped over to a nearby drugstore and scanned the bookracks. Nothing. Then, for some unknown reason, Winkle dug past the front layer of books on one rack and found a neat paperback with the compelling title *Strange Creatures from Time and Space* in canary yellow on a somber violet-blue background. A Fawcett Gold Medal book written by someone named John A. Keel, it featured a fantastic cover painting by Frank Frazetta. Winkle plunked down his six bits and spent the evening reading.

Winkle had never heard of the Mothman of West Virginia, or of the Beast of Bungay, or of the Men-in-Black who harassed UFO witnesses. Winkle had never heard of the Burning Man of Germany, or of Thomas the Winged Cat, or of the Bigfoot-type creatures reported from such unlikely places as New Jersey and Florida. Far from being knowledgeable about these strange creatures, Winkle was merely a novice.

But since that time, he has read about all manner of things, from werewolves and vampires to dinosaurs that may yet roam the earth, from objects and entities that may come from outer space, to poltergeists and tulpas that have their origin in the basement of the human psyche. When Keel expanded his account of the "Mothman" into a book of its own in 1975, Winkle was first in line at the local library.

But eventually, Winkle realized there was a problem with *The Mothman Prophecies*. "A troubling aspect of many books on unexplained phenomena," explains Winkle, "is their lack of references. Keel—and/or his faceless New York editors—left out many details and most sources for events that happened beyond Keel's personal experiences and interviews. This is a tradition that stretches back to such efforts as C. B. Colby's *Strangely Enough!*, Frank Edwards' *Stranger than Science*, and many paperbacks by Brad Steiger, Daniel Cohen, and Bernhardt J. Hurwood. Indeed, it is not limited to the paranormal. Researchers into the Ripper murders of 1888 find that earlier books on the subject give few sources beyond obvious publications like the *London Times*. The popular scientific essays of Isaac Asimov often lack references. The idea is that these are 'popular' books read for entertainment, and the general public would cringe from dreary footnotes and long bibliographies. Those more deeply interested in the subjects covered are left to track down sources themselves."

Perhaps that is the true reason for Winkle's decision to annotate John Keel's masterwork. He hopes that his effort has captured information that will expand upon the curious narrative of *The Mothman Prophecies*.

We are lucky that Winkle decided to channel his interest in Keel into the annotations he is allowing me to share with my readers. (See Appendix A.) Enjoy this insightful adventure.

CHAPTER 4

The Movie:
Successful, Sinister, and Symbolic

Hollywood's version of John Keel's masterpiece appeared in 2002. The movie, *The Mothman Prophecies*, is still being discussed in cryptozoology, the occult, and film circles. Just how the movie came about is an interesting story in itself. It began, of course, with John A. Keel's book, *The Mothman Prophecies*, which was first published in 1975. It is hard to believe today, but for almost the next two decades the book didn't get much attention. Then in October of 1991, IllumiNet Press, a small and now out-of-business publisher, reprinted the book. It is this edition that screenwriter Richard Hatem "discovered" in an old bookstore on March 16, 1997.

Struck by insomnia one night, Hatem had drifted into a Pasadena bookstore. That's when a used copy of *The Mothman Prophecies* almost literally fell from a shelf into his hands, as if guided to him by a "library angel," as these synchronistic events are called. Hatem soon was engaged in reading Keel's book through the night. Hatem "realized [that] 'true paranormal' writing had its own Hunter S. Thompson, and that person was John Keel," he recalled later.

The next day, Hatem contacted John Keel. Hatem said that Keel told him "about how Sun Classic International Pictures had tried to film 'Mothman' back in the mid-70s without ever securing the rights from him. According to the story he told me, principal photography had already started before a friend of his in Los Angeles heard about it and alerted him. Keel's lawyer, a tough bulldog of a guy with the fantastic name Knox Berger shut them down. So here it was 20 years later and at least this time someone was actually trying to secure the rights FIRST. Based on our phone call, John agreed to option the book to me."

Hatem immediately began work on the screenplay that Lakeshore Entertainment bought in 1998.

The movie would be directed by Mark Pellington, who was then known for his conspiracy thriller *Arlington Road* and award-winning MTV videos. Released to theaters in 2002, *The Mothman Prophecies* follows John Klein, played by Richard Gere, as he leaves his Washington newspaper job to investigate sightings of winged creatures referred to as "Mothman" in a small West Virginia town.

The film claims to be based on actual events that occurred in Point Pleasant, West Virginia, between November 1966 and December 1967, but it is only loosely based on John Keel's book. It is clearly a fictionalized narrative of actual events.

The characters' names were created from parts of the personality and experiences of John Keel, who thoroughly enjoyed the film and was touched to see his name on the screen. He never thought his work would be immortalized in film. He also enjoyed the little bit of money he earned from the studio, although this late in his life (he was then 72), it didn't change his lifestyle. Because he was having major health issues and eye problems at the time, I was asked to come on board to help promote the movie. The studio wanted my help in reinforcing the tagline of their feature film—"based on a true story." John and I appear as the "Mothman experts" in *Search for the Mothman,* the documentary bundled with the deluxe DVD version of the film, more about which later in this book.

The movie still draws high praise more than a decade after its release. For Halloween in 2013, the *Huffington Post* published a list of recommended Halloween horror movies, and included *The Mothman Prophecies* in their list of the top 13. The movie is a creepy one and worth reviewing again, as it has many layers of meanings and a few inside jokes, ranging from the selection of the characters' names to some of its on-camera appearances.

The Name Game
The writers had fun with the script, and the film is a series of in-jokes. For example, author John Alva Keel was born Alva John Kiehle, and the first "John Keel" character in the movie is named "John Klein," played by Richard Gere. The Alan Bates' character, Alexander Leek, is "Keel" spelled backwards. [Screenwriter Richard Hatem had so much fun with this name game in the Mothman film, he continued it in the television series he created the following year, *Miracles* (characterized by critics as a "spiritual *X-Files*"). Hatem named a character in *Miracles* after John Keel's first name at birth combined with his changed, taken name: "Alva Keel."]

In the movie, the part of the chemical plant worker named "Gordon Smallwood" is loosely based on a real life contactee named Woody Derenberger, who reported encounters with an Indrid Cold in West Virginia during the period of the Mothman sightings there in 1966–1967. Right after the movie's opening, Jerome Clark, author of *The UFO Book*, posted the following on an online UFO group: "I wonder how many of you who've seen the movie caught the deep-inside-the-ufological-beltway use of the name 'Gordon Smallwood' for the Will Patton character?" No one answered, but many were interested in learning what the in-joke was all about. Clark explained: "Gordon Smallwood is a pseudonym Gray Barker [the late West Virginia ufologist and friend of John A. Keel] used for Quebec ufologist Laimon Mitris, who allegedly was visited by a man in black. In *They Knew Too Much About Flying Saucers*, Barker writes, 'I would like to know someone by the name of Gordon Smallwood. The name in itself sounds honest and reputable. If there are any Gordon Smallwoods reading this book, let them rest assured the name used here is an invention. But let them write to me for I would like to know people with such a name.'"

The imposing figure of the bartender at the Marriott who helps the Richard Gere character with the television channels is director Mark Pellington in his Alfred Hitchcock-like cameo. Pellington was also the voice of Indrid Cold during the phone call. He also occasionally added his voice under the dialogue of characters who spoke on the phone with John Klein, throughout *The Mothman Prophecies*. Pellington said the intention was to create the illusion that Indrid Cold could be any one of those people, and that the entire situation and all the people might actually be in Klein's head.

On October 28, 2013, the film's screenwriter, Richard Hatem, posted a tweet saying, "Thanks Loren—I knew guys like you would get the jokes."

Some were not jokes, however. The clock radio in character John Klein's motel room reads: 6:14. This is a biblical reference to John Chapter 6, verse 14, which reads, "This is indeed the prophet who is to come into the world."

There is something red in every scene of the film.

Oops!

Other than the name games, the movie also had some strange errors. Continuity and geographic errors often happen in movies. It is just curious to notice the ones that pop up throughout this celluloid classic.

In the movie, you can see an obvious Pittsburgh landmark, the Masonic Temple, home of the Pitt Alumni Association, appearing in the background of scenes supposedly set in Washington, DC, and Chicago. The Richard Gere character passes a sign for Maine Avenue as he leaves Washington D.C., driving from Memorial Bridge to Interstate 95. Maine Avenue is in the opposite direction and there are no signs for Maine Avenue on any of the roads he could have taken to get to I-95.

The Richard Gere character allegedly goes to Chicago to talk to the Mothman expert played by Alan Bates, but it shows the two walking into the Mellon Institute, which is actually in Pittsburgh.

During the Christmas tree lighting festivities in Point Pleasant, West Virginia, the door of the fire truck reads "Saxonburg," a town near Kittanning in Pennsylvania where the scene was filmed. On Klein's drive from Point Pleasant to Chicago, a glimpse of an exit sign for "New Kensington" can be seen. There is no "New Kensington" between West Virginia and Illinois, but there is one near Pittsburgh, where the movie was shot.

The Movie Was Fiction

While the movie was based on John Keel's book of the same name, the film was heavily fictionalized. It was based on factual incidents, but when it became a contemporary story, not a vintage docudrama, it left reality behind rather quickly.

The number of deaths from the collapse of the bridge in the movie was less than in the history of the Silver Bridge collapse. The film has 36 people dying in the collapse of the Silver Bridge that followed all the Mothman sightings, not 46, but the studio didn't "want to kill too many," director Mark Pellington told *USA Today* in 2002. "My father's football number was 36, and 40 was too many." But 46 did die when the so-called "Mothman prophecy" occurred and the Silver Bridge collapsed. The movie also minimized the number of Mothman witnesses, left out many UFO sightings and Men-In-Black encounters, and made no mention of cattle mutilations or other weird happenings.

In the movie, news articles about the 1953 "Houston Batman" were flashed on the screen as the character "Alexander Leek" (remember, this is "Keel" backwards, but Keel never make this connection) talked about how Mothmen were seen before disasters like "the hurricane" of 1969 in Galveston and Chernobyl. But this is poor mythmaking; it is pure cryptofiction time-traveling. A blogger named Ha'ri pondered about specific details in the film in a 2009 post entitled "Mothman – Sighting in Galveston?" She wondered if any large bird-like somethings were seen before any hurricanes had hit the coastal Texas city of Galveston. Ha'ri did some research and came to the conclusion that there was nothing to be easily found about a 1969 hurricane—or Mothman sightings there. The famed big hurricanes in Galveston occurred in 1900 and 1915, long before the Houston Batman was seen in 1953.

The movie also tried to link Chernobyl's nuclear meltdown with precursor sightings of Mothman. Again, not true. There were no sightings. These were all created fictions for the movie.

These fictionalized additions to the Mothman story have long distracted researchers from any real investigations of the Point Pleasant phenomena and its real zoological underpinnings.

CHAPTER 5

The Aftermath:
Diabolical Demises, Devilish Deaths,
and Dastardly Departures

"In the end it all came down to just one simple question. Which was more important: having proof, or being alive? Trust me. I turned away years ago, and I've never looked back."

—Alexander Leek character,
THE MOTHMAN PROPHECIES, 2002.

Soon after the movie made its appearance, I began to notice a number of people were talking about the evil that seemed to surround the film. People associated with Mothman and the movie were dying. Yes, accidents do occur, and deaths are expected over time. But something more seemed to be happening here.

Of course, we have heard about such things before. Many Hollywood movies—particularly horror films, not surprisingly—are said to be cursed, including *The Exorcist, The Crow, Atuk, The Conqueror, The Omen, Rebel Without a Cause, Rosemary's Baby, Superman,* and *Apocalypse Now.* But perhaps the best-known example of a curse attached to a film is the one related to the *Poltergeist* film trilogy and its crews. It all began with the deaths of two young cast members in the six years between the release of the first and third films.

A total of five rather unusual deaths have been associated with the three *Poltergeist* films. Dominique Dunne, who played the eldest daughter Dana in the first film, died on November 4, 1982, at age 22 after being strangled by her abusive former boyfriend. Heather O'Rourke, who played Carol Anne in all three *Poltergeist* films, died on February 1, 1988 at the age of 12 due to complications from an acute bowl obstruction. Julian Beck, the evil preacher from *Poltergeist II* (1986), suffered from advanced stomach cancer during filming and died on September 14, 1985, soon after the filming was completed. Lou Perryman, age 67, who had a bit part as a construction worker in the original *Poltergeist*, was the victim of a random killing at his home in Austin, Texas. And Will Sampson, who played the spiritual Native American in *Poltergeist II* (1986), was a real-life shaman and 100% Muscogee. He was upset over the curse on the set and delayed production for hours to perform a Muscogee (Creek) blessing to clear the filming site of Evil. It seems not to have worked. He perished less than a year later, at the age of 53, from complications from a kidney failure, after a heart and lung transplant, on June 3, 1987.

Is there a similar Mothman curse? I began looking at all the deaths associated with the Mothman sightings, Silver Bridge collapse, the investigations, the books, and the films, and the horizon appeared filled with many more deaths than two or five. Since it has become fashionable to create lists of those who have died by association to the JFK assassination, to other politicians, and the *Poltergeist* movies, I began compiling "The Mothman Death List" beginning with the original series of Mothman sightings of 1966–1967, to the release of the blockbuster movie in January 2002, to the various cable premieres, and the VHS/DVD releases later in 2002 and 2003. Just a year after the movie was released, I came up with a list of more than 80 people for the "Mothman curse." Yes, some of those who died were old, and those linked to Mothman are growing older. But several were victims of youthful deaths and bizarre passings. I have now updated the list, and for the first time ever, this book contains the complete list of Mothman-related deaths, up through August of 2017.

Even John Keel may have had an inkling of what would follow. In 1975, he wrote in *The Mothman Prophecies* that "there would be many changes in the lives of those touched by" Mothman, and a "few would even commit suicide." The people he alluded to with these words remain unidentified, but I have gathered information on the hundred souls who seem tied to the events radiating out of Point Pleasant. I'm sure there are probably more.

Is Mothman responsible for this evil? Read Appendix B: The Mothman Death List, and you be the judge.

CHAPTER 6

The Town:
Curse, Collapse, and Celebration

Forty-miles down the Ohio River from Huntington, West Virginia, where the Ohio meets the Kanawha River lies Point Pleasant, West Virginia, the town "Where History and Rivers Meet." The ironic name of "Point Pleasant" was bestowed on this location since at least 1749, when the French laid claim over the Ohio Valley and buried a lead plaque at the place they called "Point Pleasant."

But bad luck followed in the wake of the French, with the local tribes remaining loyal to the British. This all ended poorly for the French, in the loss of New France, and the final defeat of France in the French and Indian War (1754–1763).

In the Battle of Point Pleasant (October 10, 1774), fought on the future site of the town, more than one thousand Virginia militiamen, led by Colonel Andrew Lewis (1720–1781), defeated a roughly equal force of an Algonquin confederation of Shawnee and Mingo warriors led by Shawnee Chief Cornstalk (ca. 1720–1777). The event is celebrated locally as the "First Battle of the American Revolutionary War."

"Camp Point Pleasant" was established in the 1770s by Colonel Lewis for his troops, and was followed by whites settling on the site. A stockade named Fort Blair was built there and was soon replaced by a new fort, Fort Randolph. Fort Randolph is best remembered as the place where Chief Cornstalk was murdered in 1777. Cornstalk was on a diplomatic mission to the military base but was detained by the fort's commander. When on November 10, an American militiaman was killed near the fort, angry soldiers brutally executed the Chief, his son, and other Shawnees. Part of the legend of the area is that due to the outrageous killing of Cornstalk in 1777, the place was laid under a curse for a hundred years. Fort Randolph withstood attack by Indians the following year, but it was abandoned in 1779.

Indians did not like this section of the wilderness. It was known for adversity and misfortune. Even Daniel Boone, who lived in and around Point Pleasant from 1786 to 1795, finally abandoned the area, when he and his family moved on to Kentucky.

The settlement at Point Pleasant did not receive an official charter until 1794 and was not named a county seat until Mason County was carved out of Kanawha County in 1804. Point Pleasant was incorporated in 1833.

From the beginning, Point Pleasant was a small village. The main industries were fur-trading and military housing, and then after 1840, boat building. Forty years after incorporation, the population still numbered less than 800.

About a hundred years later, Point Pleasant, West Virginia, became the focus of the Mothman sightings and related events. It had a population just under 6,000 in the early 1960s, before the Mothman events, and just over 6,000 by 1970. After that, people began leaving the town. In the 2010s, the population has hovered in the low 4,000s.

During the 1960s, the town's declining economy affected the business community, homes, and infrastructure. John Keel captured the gloominess of the Point Pleasant area in the novel-like opening to *The Mothman Prophecies* (1975): "Fingers of lightning tore holes in the black skies as an angry cloudburst drenched the surrealistic landscape. It was 3 a.m. on a cold, wet morning in late November 1967, and the little houses scattered along the dirt road winding through the hills of West Virginia were all dark. Some seemed unoccupied and in the final stages of decay. Others were unpainted, neglected, forlorn. The whole setting was like the opening scene of a Grade B horror film from the 1930s." So begins Keel's essay on a place that seemed tied to being both downtrodden and out-of-luck.

Less than a decade after the events of the Mothman encounters and the Silver Bridge collapse, investigator Rick Moran visited Point Pleasant in the summer of 1978, to see what changes were taking place to the town in the wake of the bizarre incidents of 1966–1967. What he found was depressing. "Point Pleasant was a congenial little town of about 5,000 people," wrote Moran in "Point Pleasant Revisited," in *Fortean Times*, April 2002, "and still bore the scars the Silver Bridge collapse."

What Moran did not find was any sign that Mothman had become a tourist attraction in the 1970s. The same would be true of Point Pleasant in the 1980s and the 1990s. Mothman was a fading memory. And until the movie came out in 2002, the flying saucers seen in the area are what people remembered and told outsiders about more than the Mothman stories.

But a hint of what was to come could be seen in the late 1990s, with the Halloween hayrides to the TNT area. Many of the Mothman sightings occurred in the countryside outside of the town itself. During World War II, explosives had been manufactured in Point Pleasant on the site of a former game preserve, which had been converted into a TNT dump. More than a hundred white bunkers were built for military purposes. The munitions plant was closed down after the war and was turned into a wildlife preserve for many years. It is also the site for toxic waste, i.e. secretly discarded slag from a downriver atomic plant.

The bunkers were still there, though in great disrepair. They are all deserted. A few bungalows and homes have also been built in the area. It's an eerie place; it was here that Mothman had staked out its nesting grounds. So it was in the wildlife preserve and the TNT area that local businesses began to use to attract revenue. It made sense. Tours. Hayrides. All acceptable sites around Halloween worked.

I journeyed to Point Pleasant at the end of 2001 and the beginning of 2002, to survey the eyewitnesses, the location, and the mood of the town before Mark Pellington's film hit the theaters. I endured snowy roads in the Appalachian Mountains, bad food, and relatively terrible local radio stations along the way to investigate Point Pleasant.

As I drove into the quaint, sleepy, little town of Point Pleasant, I had expected to see "Home of Mothman" signs similar to those I found down the road at Flatwoods, describing that town as the "Home of the Green Monster" (seen in 1952). But Point Pleasant was eerily quiet; no signs; no tourist shops, and hardly any people on the three blocks of Main Street.

In 2001, I checked in at the Lowe Hotel—100 years old, clean, safe, and very New England-looking. It faced, across the street, a stark row of empty storefronts. The Finleys, who ran the hotel, owned a few of these properties. Ruth Finley, who ran the hotel, put me in Room 203.

After a quick breakfast, the hotel gave me directions on how to get to the infamous TNT area off Route 62. Fairgrounds Road is where the young people of 1966 would drag race their '57 Chevys. It was also the entrance to the local "Lovers' Lane."

The strange wildlife area that surrounds it is desolate and isolated. I explored the woods and watery landscape four times during my stay here in 2001–2002, and only saw two other cars—trucks, actually, with hunters (or poachers), guns, and hunting dogs. I forgot to wear orange and was viewed with caution. I did sink into waist deep water while hiking off the trail, and I was lucky not to get lost.

The location of the original 1966–1967 sightings were cordoned off with tall fences, topped with barbed wire. The old "Bird Cage," as locals called the ghostly shell of the abandoned power plant where Mothman was most frequently seen, was torn down in the mid-1990s. Apart from its foundation—and those of its surrounding, low buildings—there was nothing left of the majestic and haunting building that figures so importantly in John Keel's classic work.

I also discovered the remains of other huge buildings that don't seem to have been mentioned by prior investigators. They looked like the giant Imperial Walkers in

Stars Wars: The Empire Strikes Back, but overgrown with thorny bushes. The old concrete igloos used for storing dynamite were likewise weed-covered mounds. There is some concern that toxic and nuclear waste had seeped into the ground thereabouts, and outraged local residents rejected building a high school in the TNT because they did not wish to raise glowing children. True story.

Further into the woods, beyond the unfenced TNT area, I found the wildlife preserve where other sightings had occurred. Tire tracks, empty beer bottles, and crushed cans indicated that the area still functioned as the site of sexual and alcoholic coming-of-age rituals. More sinister, perhaps, were the dead deer carcasses, including skulls and a ribcage picked clean of flesh.

Back in town, I visited Criminal Records, a music store with a few t-shirts, including one of Mothman! It was the only store to avail itself of the Mothman legend and, as I discovered, it was Jeff Wamsley's. His new oversized Mothman book was on sale there, and it seemed, in January 2002, that something big was about to happen soon, with the movie's release.

I designed my own self-guided tour of the known Mothman sites. I re-visited, for example, the armory, the pizza joint that used to be Tiny's Drive-In, and the location of the downed Silver Bridge. I also met with David Levine, CEO of butterfly.net, who had created an interactive computer game named *Mothman.* He wanted to know what a cryptozoologist did. I returned to the TNT area one night with Levine. It was silent, evocative, secluded, and dead. We went to meet Marcella Bennett and her son Mark, who was six years old when they both saw Mothman. Both are now deceased.

I interviewed many others involved in the Mothman events, including the late Linda Scarberry. My beard confused her grandchildren; they thought I was John Keel, who was then still alive.

From my hotel room, I called and spoke at length with John Keel back in New York City. Inevitably, we had some telephone trouble as we discussed matters, mostly his awful health of late and his despair over times getting better. He didn't seem to think they would.

Most of the witnesses I was able to track down, often through contacts at local diners, the Lowe Hotel, and Criminal Records, were reflective of the poverty, mental anguish, and what appeared to be post-traumatic stress from the bridge collapse (not the Mothman sightings). But the Sony/Screen Gems film would offer a small ray of deliverance.

As January 2002 dawned, the only Chamber of Commerce plaques visible around town were those honoring Revolutionary War veterans, Chief Cornstalk's death in 1777, sheriff's deputies killed in a jail explosion in 1976, and the victims of the Silver Bridge collapse of 1976. There was not one plaque, local flyer, map, postcard, street sign, or specialty shop that mentioned or even exploited the historical significance of Mothman.

But there was a change in the wind. During the summer of 2001, for the first time in Point Pleasant's history, the Chamber of Commerce had begun producing a souvenir with a Mothman on it. Curiously, it was a Christmas ornament with a red-eyed human-looking Mothman painted on the orb. It seemed bizarre because of the direct association between the Christmas-time collapse of the Silver Bridge and Mothman.

There was also the t-shirt with a Mothman on it at Criminal Records, and a new beanie doll that Hilda Austin, the Executive Director of the Chamber of Commerce, showed me. Indeed, knowing that I was working with Sony/Screen Gems on the publicity for the forthcoming movie, members of the Chamber, owners of the Lowe Hotel, and other business people met with me in the lobby of the hotel. I told them that if what happened to Roswell, New Mexico, after the Showtime movie was any indication of what the Mothman movie might do for Point Pleasant, they should prepare to receive lots of tourists after the opening of *The Mothman Prophecies*. Roswell's museum had one million visitors in its first year. I suggested they might start thinking about a museum in one of their empty storefronts, as well as producing bumper stickers, street signs, and other Mothman-related materials to save their dying town.

The folks of Point Pleasant soon realized they had lightning in the palm of their hands. *The Mothman Prophecies* began screening around the USA on January 25, 2002. The film eventually earned a worldwide total of over $55 million. But more than that, it was repeated so often on cable networks, the story of Mothman became a living legend of weird cryptozoology, occult demonology, and banshee predictions. New fans of Mothman were born.

The town of Point Pleasant had a winner after the movie came out, and tourism was on the table. In 2002, the first Mothman Festival took root. It was a small affair, but it was a success. Today, Point Pleasant's Main Street is blocked for the Mothman festival, vendors line the street, speakers give talks in the usually closed State Theater, and bus tours visit the TNT and other areas where Mothman sighting took place. The Festival occurs on the third weekend of every September. Jeff Wamsley, his family, and diner owner Carolin Harris, who passed away recently, are acknowledged as the founders of the Festival.

In 2003, a 12-foot-tall, full-metal statue of an insectoid (versus a more realistic giant birdlike) Mothman was dedicated in the downtown square, Gunn Park, opposite the Lowe Hotel. The local artist and sculptor Bob Roach, also now deceased, made it from stainless steel. The model for the Point Pleasant giant replica is clearly reminiscent of the May 1980 *High Times* magazine cover illustration of Mothman by Frank Frazetta. This same painting is what Ron Bonds used on the cover of his 1991 IllumiNet Press edition of John Keel's *The Mothman Prophecies*. Even though the Mothman was never said to be a giant moth by any of the eyewitnesses, the imagery of Frazetta's cover art, now physically captured in Roach's sculpture, lives on in Point Pleasant—and in popular culture.

Setting the stage for the Mothman Museum was Criminal Records' infant beginnings and association with Mothman even before the 2002 movie. The Mothman Museum and Research Center opened in 2005 on the same side of the street as the Lowe Hotel. The founder, owner, and director of the museum is Jeff Wamsley. When I was in town, again in 2011, filming for a Canadian documentary, I was impressed by the changes the town had made in the decade since the movie. They had changed their tune and were fully behind the positive changes *The Mothman Prophecies* film was bringing to the tourism of the area.

The Mothman Museum grew larger and larger, and in recent years relocated to quarters in a space where two stores used to be on Main Street, directly across from the Lowe Hotel. When I returned again in 2016, the improvements to the small downtown were visibly noticeable. By 2016 and 2017, the Mothman Festival had evolved into an enormous street fair and lecture series. Large, souvenir-seeking crowds visited the Festival for the 50th Anniversary of the initial Mothman visitations in 2016, when I gave a keynote talk.

Mothman still has its doubters, including one person who approached Point Pleasant Councilman Rick Simpkins and complimented Jeff Wamsley's efforts but who felt the Mothman wasn't real. According to the Point Pleasant *Daily Register* of September 13, 2017, Simpkins told the doubter: "I don't care if he's real or not but the festival's real and brings 10,000 people to my town."

For those who wish to know and "experience" Mothman for themselves, there will always be one and only one town to visit—Point Pleasant.

CHAPTER 7

The Documentaries:
Truth, Tragedy, and Trust

The release of *The Mothman Prophecies* by Sony/Screen Gem in 2002 has led several documentary filmmakers to look into the reality behind the theatrical release. Several reality television programs have attempted to look into the Mothman question, as well. Here are details on three formal documentaries and one example of a "documentary" from a television series.

Search for the Mothman (David Grabias, 2002)
This 44-minute documentary about the Mothman of West Virginia was directed by David Grabias, funded by Sony/Screen Gems, and included on the special edition DVD of major motion picture *The Mothman Prophecies*, released on January 25, 2002. The Grabias documentary was broadcast on FX on January 23, 2002.

The documentary contains many interviews with Mothman witnesses and Point Peasant residents, as well as archive footage from 1966–1967. John A. Keel and I are the two major Mothman historians appearing throughout. Keel, author of *The Mothman Prophecies*, is featured in the documentary to give commentary on the sightings and events based on his time in the small town during the late 1960s. I present insights into the various theories, various sites, and Native American accounts related to the film's focus on the Mothman sightings.

When I slipped into Point Pleasant in 2011, unannounced, to wait for a film crew, I was shocked to be immediately recognized all over town. I soon found out why when I went into a little souvenir shop and found *Search for the Mothman* playing constantly on a giant television monitor behind the front counter. As I walked into the store, my image was on the screen, and the owner yelled out, "Hello, Mr. Coleman."

Search for the Mothman utilizes photos of newspapers, artistic representations of the creature, and clips from the major motion picture. Unfortunately, fictional clips from the Mark Pellington movie regarding Mothman sightings before the 1986 Chernobyl accident and the 1985 Mexico City earthquake are purely mythical and are not based on facts. The documentary also repeats *The Mothman Prophecies* use of news articles about the "Houston Batman" that were flashed on the screen as the character "Alexander Leek" talked of how Mothmen were seen before disasters like "the hurricane" of 1969 in Galveston. (The Houston Batman was a huge winged man-thing reportedly seen in a pecan tree near the center of Houston, Texas, on July 18, 1953 by Mrs. Hilda Walker.) But the famed big hurricanes in Galveston occurred in 1900 and 1915, long before the Houston Batman was seen in 1953. For a documentary, this was regrettable.

Search for the Mothman is still available bundled with *The Mothman Prophecies* (Mark Pellington, 2002)—Special Edition—on Amazon Video, Blu-Ray, and DVD.

SciFi Investigates Mothman (SciFi Crew, 2006)

On October 26, 2006, a television documentary was broadcast entitled *SciFi Investigates Mothman*. (It appeared before NBCUniversal announced that SciFi was rebranding as Syfy.)

Although it had its entertaining moments and was certainly funny, it had little or nothing to do with "investigating" Mothman or unexplained phenomena. Although eyewitnesses were interviewed, sites were visited, and group discussions were recorded, the program was a forensic failure. The archival footage was interesting, but the repeating images of the collapsed bridge and recreated Mothman-in-flight scenes were visibly boring after their third time through. Did they run out of other b-roll so quickly?

The level of skepticism in this Mothman episode was neither scientific nor well-grounded. The "skeptic's" point of view was represented mostly by *Survivor's* "Boston" Rob Mariano. His ridicule was less-than-intellectual, and as purely personal opinions and feelings, they were baseless.

What may surprise people is that I think the show was not skeptical enough. It was a failure because it portrayed the most egregious elements and mistakes of the Mothman melodrama as facts, as straw men, only to then knock them down. By presenting sham arguments for the existence of Mothman, it was easy to see why the "investigators" as well as the audience would essentially mow down Mothman.

The straw men appearing in this Mothman program were so obvious as to be outrageous. The program producers appear to have not done any homework on the "cases" they were examining. The usual eyewitnesses, of course, were interviewed. And, yes, the details in the stories did change, people have elaborated their sightings, and new specifics have drifted into the retellings. It was an easy matter to see how these stories have evolved, and this would have been a worthwhile exercise. The program claimed they did this. They did not.

One of the most obvious mistakes made in *SciFi Investigates Mothman,* and repeated over and over again by eyewitnesses trying to play to the media and to television "investigators" like these, was the myth about the "glowing red eyes" of Mothman. While doing a publicity tour for Screen Gems in conjunction with the 2002 movie, I learned that the eyes did not "glow" but were reflected light. Mentioning this detail makes the stories less exciting and more zoological, so people have not liked me to point this out. Mothman researcher and skeptic Robert Goerman has reinforced the non-glowing argument in "Mothman's Eyes," which appeared on *The Anomalist* website in 2002. Goerman did what anyone looking into Mothman should do: he did what I did, he read the original reports. Here are two examples from 1966:

"...fiery-red eyes that glow when the lights hit it. There was no glowing about it until the lights hit it."

—Linda Scarberry, 1966.

"The young men said they saw the creature's eyes, which glowed red, only when their lights shined on it."

—*Point Pleasant Register*
(Wednesday, November 16, 1966)

Bioluminescence? Eyes glowing on their own? Obviously not, but you would not know this from watching this 2006 SciFi television program because it was scarier to talk about "searching the TNT for glowing red eyes!" I suppose it's boring to talk about the reality of animal eyeshine.

Needless to say, people haven't enjoyed my saying that there is no "moth" involved in these big bird reports either.

Some of the eyewitnesses have so changed their stories over the years as to disqualify them from being useful interview subjects. Since the 2002 movie appeared, the newly retold old accounts have become so changed from the originals to be almost totally useless—except as fodder for nearly fictional television programs.

SciFi Investigates Mothman had footage of divers jumping into the murky Ohio River searching for evidence of the collapsed bridge. What difference would it have made if a piece of a car that fell from the bridge in 1967 had been found? Why was this even discussed as "physical evidence" of Mothman? This was insulting to the audience and disrespectful to the victims and families of the bridge collapse. There was no logic to showing an entire scene of Boston Rob taking off his shirt, putting on a rubber suit, and diving into the river, other than to obtain sensational visuals, pure and simple. This was not an "investigation."

All kinds of phenomena—Men in Black, UFOs, Silver Bridge collapse, Lowe Hotel haunting—were thrown into the pot in *SciFi Investigates Mothman*. But the impact and influence of John Keel's investigations and his demonological philosophy were never mentioned, despite being available through his on-site interviews in 1966–1967, his 1967–1975 magazine writings, and his 1975 book. Indeed, even an analysis between the dates of the Mothman encounters and those of the UFO sightings would have shown a diversity in data distribution that did not necessarily overlap in the mythic fashion that is often recalled. *SciFi Investigates Mothman* just used Mothman to showcase the team and sell advertising. The "real" Mothman was forgotten in creating this program.

SciFi Investigates Mothman has not been repeated on television in recent years, but can be found on YouTube.

Eyes of the Mothman (Matthew J. Pellowski, 2007)

This 2-hour-and-30-minute documentary by Red Line Studios offers an in-depth look at some of the reported Mothman sightings in Point Pleasant, and deals as well with Chief Cornstalk, the TNT Area, Men in Black, the Indrid Cold story, and the Silver Bridge collapse. *Eyes of The Mothman* features some recreations of the death of Chief Cornstalk and Woodrow Derenberger's encounter with Indrid Cold.

The film took a rocky road to completion. Matt Pellowski went to the 4th Annual Mothman Festival in 2005 to start his project. The documentary reportedly finished filming in 2006 and was in post-production for at least five years. The documentary was screened for the first time at the 9th Annual Mothman Festival in 2010 and then publically released on February 22, 2011. DVDs were sold at the Mothman Museum.

People either love or hate this documentary. A few critics have said it suffers from less-than-tight editing. Others say that it presents too many theories. Some reviewers were delighted with all the eyewitness accounts. It is remarkable that such a vast gap exists between the documentary's fans and foes.

Eyes of The Mothman is available on YouTube and via online sellers.

The Mothman of Point Pleasant (Seth Breedlove, 2017)

The Small Town Monsters film company released a full-feature (67 minutes long) documentary *The Mothman of Point Pleasant* on June 2, 2017. The Ohio production group behind a series of outstanding documentaries—*Minerva Monster, Beast of Whitehall, Boggy Creek Monster*, and *Invasion on Chestnut Ridge*—has delivered another groundbreaking documentary film about cryptozoology.

Written, produced, and directed by Seth Breedlove, *The Mothman of Point Pleasant* is destined to be the yardstick against which any other attempts to capture the reality of Mothman will be measured. Listening to the narration by Lyle Blackburn, well known for his serious and thorough investigations of the Boggy Creek creatures, the viewer feels as if he or she is on an Ohio River journey through the rural history of the now-infamous Mothman.

The Mothman of Point Pleasant is a vast historic view of this epic event that today is called "Mothman." From the first overhead shots of the drone cinematography by Zachary Palmisano, showing the poverty-filled landscape of the area, to Brandon Dalo's haunting music that reflects the devastated surroundings, the film gives a sense of foreboding in Point Pleasant.

The documentary provides a huge amount of detail and leaves us wondering why no one told us before that so much was happening. Breedlove's use of a time chart as a thread throughout the film helps the observer get a grip on the two years of visceral terror that existed right below the surface of this small town. The use of newsreel footage and interviews with eyewitnesses and locals are powerful pivotal points that anchor the viewer, even those who already know the story well. Breedlove's film builds to a crescendo, and one just hopes, for once, it isn't the one we all know is coming. Maybe, just this once, history was an illusion, and the Silver Bridge collapse didn't really happen.

But it does, and Jeff Wamsley's father's original old footage of the aftermath of the Silver Bridge collapse graphically shows what few have seen. This evocative material is poignant and well handled by Breedlove.

The film shares a deep, thoughtful, human moment about Mothman, which is often forgotten in sensationalized television reality programming about strange creatures. It is voiced by Lawrence Gary, a schoolteacher who had his own encounter with Mothman some 50 years ago. It shook him to such an extent he questioned his own guilt in bringing this upon himself. "Lord, what did I do? This Thing is here. This evil presence... It is evil. 100% evil," says Lawrence Gary to the camera.

Indeed, what brought the Mothman to this existence, what was its purpose, why do we even have to have it in our awareness? *The Mothman of Point Pleasant* provides viewers exactly what they need to ponder such questions.

Richard Hatem, screenwriter of the movie *The Mothman Prophecies*, watched the documentary and wrote to Seth Breedlove early in September 2017: "I wanted to let you know that I finally watched your film—just now—and I think it's incredible. It's completely enthralling. Haunting and eerie, but full of heart and humanity. I loved the interviews with the original witnesses and the footage from the aftermath of the actual bridge collapse—this material I've never seen. In fact, I was surprised at the amount of detail and information that I was hearing for the first time. You really got to the human heart of the mystery. The whole tone of the thing is just perfect; mournful, unsettling yet also oddly beautiful. All my favorite things."

Seth Breedlove has shared with me some observations and insights on his 2017 documentary:

"On a blustery, cold afternoon in December of 1967, the Silver Bridge in Point Pleasant, West Virginia fell into the icy waters of the Ohio River. Fifty years later, on the eve of the anniversary of the incident, I found myself in downtown Point Pleasant filming b-roll on our first day of production for our movie, *The Mothman of Point Pleasant*.

"There's something to be said about synchronicity and the Mothman. Not simply relating to strange dates or names or deaths, but to bizarre, seemingly-inconsequential happenings as well. For instance, I recall my first experience seeing *The Mothman Prophecies* in a movie theater in 2002. I saw the movie with my friend, Zac Palmisano and a handful of others, and can recall enjoying it to some degree. A week later, after pondering its deeper meaning and engaging in multiple conversations regarding the titular characters lack of a presence, I went back. And then I went back again, and again, and probably again still. I became something of a fanboy for that film. So much so that when I found a worn, paperback copy of a book bearing the same name by some guy named John Keel in my sister's room later that same year, I eagerly opened it. What I discovered was a years-long investigation into the unknown that opened my eyes to the paranormal, and served as a crash-course introduction into a subject I would one day find myself completely enamored with.

"But, I digress. The synchronicity here comes from that first experience seeing *The Mothman Prophecies*, as fifteen years later I found myself on the streets of the real Point Pleasant (rather than the fictional one glimpsed in that film) working away with Zac Palmisano on our own Mothman movie. On this very same evening I also met Carolin Harris for the first time. Carolin, of course was known as the 'matriarch of Main Street' and was renowned for owning Harris' Steakhouse: home of the world-famous Mothman Burger.

"Carolin had lost loved ones in the bridge collapse, but years later found the bright side of that incident by helping to pull her town from the brink of financial collapse when she helped establish the Mothman itself as a sort of local icon. Despite the Mothman's legendary connection to the Silver Bridge incident, Carolin had embraced the story and over decades had assisted Jeff Wamsley with the local Mothman Festival; an event that attracts thousands to the town. I tumbled into her diner on that cold December night for a brief visit to escape the cold, while Zac continued to dutifully shoot the darkened streets outside.

"Carolin was warm, welcoming, and all the things a documentarian looks for in a subject. She was open about her past and emotional in even recounting the smaller aspects of the incidents that transpired at the height of the Mothman craze of 1966-67. I remember her telling me for no real reason that her favorite restaurant was a nigh-obsolete fast food chain called 'Rax,' and that she was planning a trip to the only remaining location soon. We spoke for a few minutes, and in that time the heretofore fuzzy details of how I was going to stylistically approach my own Mothman movie began to come into focus for me. Carolin helped clarify the whole thing for me.

"On the drive home that night, I talked extensively with Zac about the look of the film; now envisioned as a sort of hand-held day-to-day look at the citizens of Point Pleasant, and how people live in a place where the bizarre defines the community. Then Carolin passed away. Shortly after Christmas I got the phone call that one of our key players in the legend was no more and suddenly the whole game was changed.

"As a filmmaker, I'm weirdly accustomed to this: adjusting our story and storytelling style on the fly and figuring out ways around obstacles that pop up at random. However, what Carolin's passing did for me, and for the entire tone of the film, was to illustrate something that is becoming more and more apparent to me with each project. Carolin's death was a much-needed reminder that time is stealing these stories from us, and if someone like Loren Coleman isn't out there documenting them, they will be lost.

"*The Mothman of Point Pleasant* production was a relatively smooth affair. We suffered through some miserably cold shooting days (a product of filming in January and February), and had to find some work-arounds to bizarre technical hurdles connected to the camera we decided to shoot with, but nothing stood out as extraordinary. During the ramp-up to the shoot I was consistently being told we would face untold horrors while filming. Technical glitches, batteries draining without warning, possible fatal accidents...The Mothman Curse would get us.

"No, I never saw evidence of a curse. What I did find was a lovely little town on the banks of the Ohio River and a beautiful legend that I got to play a small part in. I did find synchronicity in playing a part in a story that I'd fallen in love with fifteen years before when it played on that dollar theater movie screen while sitting next to my best pal.

"I now realize I didn't write much about the Mothman itself in the documentary. Maybe that's due to the fact that I've never considered this the creature's story as much as the people it has haunted. People like Carolin Harris, Marcella Bennett, or Thomas Ury. At the end of the day, all the bizarre, otherworldly activity associated with these stories melts away, and we're left with the memories of the individuals who played a part in them. I hope that if anyone takes anything away from the documentary, it's the profound importance of remembering our past."

As a counterpoint to Seth Breedlove's positive overview of his filming of his Mothman documentary, I must share what Breedlove freely shared on Facebook late in the summer of 2017. Just as Seth Breedlove was rolling out premieres of his new Mothman documentary, his wife was diagnosed with a tumor on her liver. Weeks and weeks of anguish and worry followed for the Breedloves, and while they did not see any link between the Mothman post-production work he was doing, others may. The Mothman curse has a way of sneaking up on you, when you least expect it.

The Mothman of Point Pleasant premiered at various locations around the country in 2017, including for the first time in New England over Labor Day Weekend at the International Cryptozoology Conference, where Seth Breedlove was bestowed The Cryptozoologist of the Year 2017 award. The film was also shown at the 16th Annual Mothman Festival, in September 2017.

The Mothman of Point Pleasant is available from online bookstores, at the International Cryptozoology Museum bookstore, and directly from the website of Small Town Monsters at smalltownmonsters.com.

Gallery: People, Places, and Pictures

The late John A. Keel was the primary investigator, chronicler, and spokesperson on the Mothman phenomena.

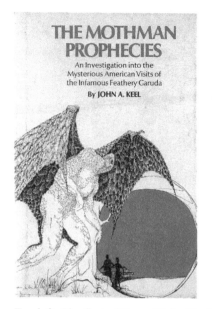

Top left: The first edition of John Keel's *The Mothman Prophecies* appeared from Saturday Review Press in 1975.

Credit: Saturday Review Press

Top right: Publisher Ron Bonds' IllumiNet Press published the 1991 edition of *The Mothman Prophecies*. The book's cover used the Frank Frazetta Mothman artwork from the cover of *High Times* #57, May 1980. This insect-like depiction of Mothman became the inspiration for the statue in downtown Point Pleasant, West Virginia.

Credit: IllumiNet

Left: Re-published in conjunction with the release of the Sony/Screen Gems movie of the same name in 2002, the Tor edition of *The Mothman Prophecies* was unique in having a newly written "Afterword" by John A. Keel. Readers found Keel's closing statement to be "crusty."

Credit: Tor Books

Michael D. Winkle is the researcher and author of "The Mothman Annotations" (Appendix A), which has been a lifelong passion of his.

Credit: Michael D. Winkle

RIGHTENED OBSERVERS—Four young Point Pleasant residents return to ie spot where an unusual creature was spotted earlier this week. The married ouples, Mr. and Mrs. Steve Mallette, left, and Mr. and Mrs. Roger Scarberry nsiend they found a "hoof-like" print in soft sand the next day. Staff Photo by ieorge Lovell.

The media-acknowledged "first eyewitnesses" of Mothman seen near Point Pleasant, West Virginia, on November 15, 1966, were Roger and Linda Scarberry, and Steve and Mary Mallette. In varying degrees, they were touched by the Mothman curse. (Appendix B) Notice the shadowy 5th figure in the background? That's Gary "Lonnie" Button, Steve Mallette's cousin, who was along in the '57 Chevy during that "first" encounter. But he's never been interviewed, nor does anyone know what happened to him.

Credit: The Athens Messenger

The newspaper front page reads:

Charleston Daily Mail FINAL EDITION

Bridge Disaster Toll May Reach 46; Shocked Pt. Pleasant Seeking Dead

Loaded With Cars, Big Span To Ohio Collapses In River

Town's Mayor Warned SRC Of Weak Span

TWISTED GIRDERS SHROUDING LONELY PIER TELL TRAGIC STORY OF SILVER BRIDGE COLLAPSE

FEARS RAISED IN CITY
What About 2 Old Charleston Spans?

School Bonds Voter Turnout Starting Light

—SLITHERED LIKE A SNAKE—
'Mommy, Mommy, Look, The Bridge Is Falling'

After the Silver Bridge collapsed on December 15, 1967, the local newspapers kept shocked residents informed daily of developments in the unfolding tragedy and death toll.

Credit: Charleston Daily Mail

Workers spent weeks attempting to recover bodies from the Ohio River. Forty-six people died when the Silver Bridge collapsed on December 15, 1967. Two victim's bodies were never found.

Credit: State of West Virginia, Department of Highway

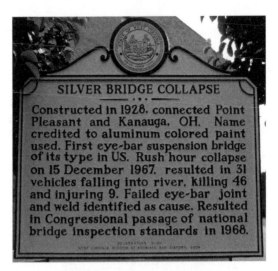

SILVER BRIDGE COLLAPSE

Constructed in 1928, connected Point Pleasant and Kanauga, OH. Name credited to aluminum colored paint used. First eye-bar suspension bridge of its type in US. Rush hour collapse on 15 December 1967, resulted in 31 vehicles falling into river, killing 46 and injuring 9. Failed eye-bar joint and weld identified as cause. Resulted in Congressional passage of national bridge inspection standards in 1968.

The State of West Virginia placed a tourist information plaque in Point Pleasant to inform visitors of the 1967 Silver Bridge disaster.

Credit: West Virginia Division of Archives and History

Reporter Mary Hyre may have been the first post-Silver Bridge "Mothman Curse" death. She died on February 15, 1970. She was deeply involved with John Keel's investigations in West Virginia, and he was startled and shocked by her passing.

Credit: Athens Messenger

Top left: Fred Freed, 53, executive producer and writer of documentary news programs for NBC, was found mysteriously dead on March 31, 1974, at his Fifth Avenue home in New York City. Freed had been working with John Keel on a special news documentary on Mothman, but his death stopped all pre-production.

Credit: NBC

Top right: California screenwriter and producer Richard Hatem discovered the 1991 edition of *The Mothman Prophecies* late one night in 1997. Interested and intrigued, he went on to write the screenplay for the movie which was released in 2002.

Credit: Richard Hatem

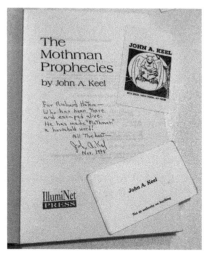

John Keel forever appreciated Hatem's discovery of his book, and thanked him for what become a successful coincidence.

Credit: Richard Hatem

Alan Bates (as "Alexander Leek," Keel spelled backwards) and Richard Gere (as "John Klein," a play on John Keel's birth name, "Keihle") starred as two parts of John Keel's personality in their fictional characters. John Keel told screenwriter Richard Hatem that he genuinely enjoyed the jokes that Richard Gere had been cast to play him because they looked alike. But, in truth, Hatem says, Keel looked more like Bates, who basically played the other side of John Keel in the movie.

Credit: Sony/Screen Gems

John Keel and Loren Coleman worked together and separately on parts of the Mothman mystery for four decades. Coleman assisted Keel with the publicity for the film in 2002, when Keel became gravely ill and nearly blind.

Credit: Patrick Huyghe

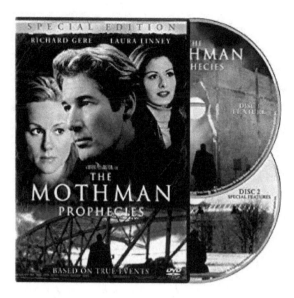

The Mothman Prophecies Special Edition DVD contained the documentary *Search for the Mothman*, containing commentary by John Keel, Loren Coleman, and several of the original eyewitnesses.

Credit: Sony/Screen Gems

Ohio filmmaker Seth Breedlove and the crew of Small Town Monsters captured the reality of the melodrama of the events in West Virginia in 1966–1967 in his documentary *The Mothman of Point Pleasant*.

Credit: Seth Breedlove/ Small Town Monsters

Top left: *The Mothman of Point Pleasant*, released in June 2017, was directed, written, produced, and edited by Seth Breedlove, co-written and narrated by Lyle Blackburn, photographed by Zachary Palmisano, and with music by Brandon Dalo.

Credit: Seth Breedlove/Small Town Monsters

Top right: Lon Strickler of Pennsylvania is the primary investigator of the current Chicago Mothman sightings.

Credit: Lon Strickler

Milwaukee researchers Allison Jornlin (right) and Kimberly Poeppey (left) traveled to the Windy City and investigated the Chicago Mothman accounts in late summer 2017. Jornlin's work is ongoing.

Credit: Allison Jornlin and Kimberly Poeppey

Top left: Jeff Wamsley founded the Mothman Museum, and cofounded with Carolin Harris, the Mothman Festival.

Credit: Jeff Wamsley

Top right: Carolin Harris first opened the Harris Steakhouse in 1969. It was known locally as the "Mothman Diner." She ran it until she passed away in 2016. Harris also co-founded the Mothman Festival with Jeff Wamsley and other Point Pleasant business people.

Credit: Loren Coleman

Left: Everyone becomes a cryptotourist in front of the iconic Mothman statue in Gunn Park, Point Pleasant, West Virginia. Author Loren Coleman and his wife, Jenny, take their turn during the Mothman Festival in 2016.

Credit: Loren Coleman

Acknowledgements

My sincere thanks to everyone mentioned in *Mothman and Other Curious Encounters* (2002) and noted throughout the text of this book, plus deep appreciation for the support and *patience* given by Jenny, Patrick, Alex, Jeff, Jeremy, Caleb, Malcolm, Fergus, Seth, Michael, Claudio, Richard, and Mark, in finishing this companion volume. Could not have done it without you, folks.

Further Reading

The Mothman Prophecies is not John Keel's only book by any means. He is also well known for his groundbreaking book on UFOs entitled *Operation Trojan Horse*, and its follow-up *The Eighth Tower*. Many people were introduced to his writings with *Jadoo*, the tale of Keel's Indiana Jones-like adventures through the mysterious world that was once known as the "Orient." There are other John Keel books as well, including some that are compilations of his magazine articles.

We hear that Rosemary Ellen Guiley and Karl Petry are considered writing a biography of John Keel. We very much hope that project comes to fruition.

If you are interested in updates on the Mothman-related events in Chicago, follow the work of Lou Strickler at phantomsandmonsters.com.

And if you want to keep up with insights into the work of John Keel, there is no better place than the website created by his good friend, Doug Skinner. You can find it at JohnKeel.com.

If you make a trip to Point Pleasant, you will want to visit the Mothman Museum (mothmanmuseum.com), where you will find various Mothman videos and books by Jeff Wamsley on sale.

Finally, I invite you to read my 2002 book, *Mothman and Other Curious Encounters*, as well as come to the International Cryptozoology Museum in Portland, Maine, where you can view some Mothman-related artifacts and exhibits. I'm often on hand to talk to patrons about the legacy and latest on the winged weirdies. For more information on directions to the Museum or buying autographed books, see cryptozoologymuseum.com.

Appendix A:
THE MOTHMAN ANNOTATIONS

By Michael D. Winkle

The page numbers of these annotations refer to the Tor Books reprint of *The Mothman Prophecies* by John A. Keel, the version most easily obtainable by the general public. These page numbers generally follow closely in other editions of the book.

CHAPTER ONE

Page 1: The "Beelzebub" scene was more-or-less recreated in the film *The Mothman Prophecies*. Rather than coming this late in the "Year of the Garuda," it became Richard Gere's character's introduction to Point Pleasant.

Page 3: Long hair = superintellectual. I can just hear Foghorn Leghorn: "Hey, boy! Put down that *long-hair* book!" By coincidence, I recently flipped through a book written in the 1850s that made light of a meeting of Spiritualists, who were constantly referred to as "a bunch of long-hairs," indicating the phrase is at least a century and a half old. Nowadays, of course, one would think hippies.

Page 5: "shelved maybe fifty others..." Considering how many people Keel interviewed and weird events he reported in his articles and books, his total case load must have been staggering.

Coincidences: Charles Fort was leery of them: "In the explanation of coincidence there is much of laziness, and helplessness, and response to an instinctive fear that a scientific dogma will be endangered." (*Wild Talents*, Chapter Two.)

"... irritatingly complex medical and psychological theories..." An indication that Keel is promoting what is known as the Psychosocial Theory here rather than the Ultraterrestrial or Window theories.

Page 6: "Mental telepathy is now a tested and verified phenomenon." Other writers have made sweeping statements like this. I'm sure there is evidence enough to convince many researchers that psi phenomena are real, but obviously, such powers are not accepted by the scientific establishment.

Tulpas: The most famous tulpa story comes from Alexandra David-Neel's *Magic and Mystery in Tibet*. A lama of eastern Tibet told Ms. David-Neel: "What becomes of these creations? May it not be that like children born of our flesh, these children of our mind separate their lives from ours, escape our control, and play parts of their own?" (pp. 147–148 of the Penguin edition)
     The idea of a *tulpa* "Shadow" on the loose is certainly intriguing.

Page 7: Archeological sites: For revisionist or Fortean speculations in archeology, one might study the Sourcebook Project volumes compiled by William Corliss, like *Ancient Man* and *Strange Artifacts*. Also, Charles Hapgood's *Maps of the Ancient Sea Kings* (1966) is one of the only "Atlantis/Lost Continent/Lost Civilization" books I ever found convincing.

Page 8: Erich von Däniken: After a meteoric rise to fame in the 1960s and 1970s, von Däniken's books have almost faded from view. While I see no reason why extraterrestrials could not have influenced earthly cultures in ancient times, von Däniken's "evidence" has proven very dubious. See *The Encyclopedia of Extraterrestrial Encounters* by Ronald D. Story, *The Space-Gods Revealed* (1976), also by Story, and "The Outer Space Confusion" in Francis Hitching's *The Mysterious World* (1978).

Ancient UFOs: Ronald Story writes: "On the walls of the famous Les Eyzies, Lascaux, and Altamira caves in France and Spain are found renderings of objects that clearly resemble modern descriptions (and photographs) of disc-shaped UFOs. Just what the Magdalenian artists were attempting to portray—15,000 to 30,000 years ago—may never be known." (Story 2001, pp. 58–59)

Keel's *Operation Trojan Horse* contains many references to UFO-like phenomena in the Bible. Zechariah 1:8–11 describes that prophet's encounter with non-human entities that can pass for humans, what Keel would call "ultraterrestrials": "I saw by night, and behold a man riding upon a red horse, and he stood among the myrtle trees that were in the bottom; and behind him there were red horses, speckled and white. Then I said, O my Lord, what are these? And the angel that talked with me said unto me, I will shew thee what these be. And the man that stood among the myrtle trees answered and said, These are they whom the Lord hath sent to walk to and fro through the earth. And they answered the angel of the Lord that stood among the myrtle trees, and said, We have walked to and fro through the earth, and, behold, all the earth sitteth still, and is at rest."

OINTs: Ivan Sanderson attempts to define "Other Intelligences" in Chapter 14 of *Invisible Residents* (1970), "Who and Where are the OINTs?" His introduction to the book seems more succinct: "Whether the 'invisible residents' are truly residents or just visitors, we don't know, but after considering the evidence, I am afraid I have to say I think they *are here*." (Sanderson, p. vi)

Page 9: "They are not from outer space." Keel says in *Operation Trojan Horse*: "... we have thousands upon thousands of UFO sightings which force two unacceptable answers upon us:

"1. *All* the witnesses were mistaken or lying.

"2. Some tremendous unknown civilization is exerting an all-out effort to manufacture thousands of different types of UFOs and is sending all of them to our planet.

"The governments of the world have seized upon variations of the first explanation. The UFO enthusiasts accept the second.

"I do not accept either one." (Keel 1970b, p. 127)

Keel's alternative is known as the Ultraterrestrial Theory; more on that and other alternatives later.

CHAPTER TWO

Page 13: "Gray Barker of Clarksburg." This name will pop up frequently later, not always under the best of circumstances.

Page 14: Rockland, Texas Airship. "1897, April 22/ [witnessed by] John M. Barclay/ *Houston Post*, 25 Apr. 1897, p. 13," according to the *Geo-Bibliography of Anomalies* by George M. Eberhart. Oddly, Daniel Cohen's book (below) mentions Barclay in the index, but I could not find him in the text.

In his book *Solving the 1897 Airship Mystery*, Michael Busby reprints the entire article from the *Houston Post*. The original article, oddly, gives the witness' name as "John Smith," possibly to protect his privacy (which indicates Barclay was a real person, not a fictional character in a hoax). This could have led to a bit of confusion, since the "inventor" calls himself Smith.

That name excites author Busby, however. His theory was that there really were secret inventors in the 1890s who actually built working airships, one of whom was a Dr. C. A. Smith, who gave an interview to a reporter from the *San Francisco Chronicle*: "A horizontal rudder of sufficient dimensions will steer the ship up or down, and a vertical rudder will steer it to right or left. Both will be on the stern. The wings will extend the full length of the cylinder and in flight will be used as aeroplanes, like the wings of the larger birds." (*San Francisco Chronicle*, November 11, 1896) Busby has identified "Smith" with a man named "Dr. Catlin" from another interview.

Busby's book is impressive; he went to the trouble of taking every Texas airship report, plotting the time, date, place, and direction of travel, and re-creating their flight patterns—patterns that simply wouldn't exist in a series of fake news stories.

Finally, I suspect this author is not the Mike Busby of Cairo, Illinois, who was attacked by a "phantom panther" in April 1970. [That is merely a "name game," issuing directly from my investigation of the 1970 Busby case. —Loren.]

Page 15: Aurora Airship. Daniel Cohen devotes a chapter to this affair in his *Great Airship Mystery* (1981).

Page 16: Eddie Webb: The news story of his nasty close encounter was sent across the country by UPI on October 5, 1973. It is reprinted whole in *Beyond Earth: Man's Contact with UFOs* (1974) by Ralph and Judy Blum.

Page 18: "… stranger in a strange land." You have to wonder: Did this guy pay his bill? Did he have to wash dishes?

Page 19: "Richard French" is expanded upon in *Operation Trojan Horse*, Chapter Ten. In November of 1966, Mrs. Butler and a friend were out in a field watching a phenomenon they had dubbed "little flashers," dancing, blinking lights that had been appearing nearly every evening. This night one of the lights dropped near to the ground at the other end of the field. Mrs. Butler's friend sank to her knees with a gasp, and she spoke in a strange, mechanical voice: "'What … is … your … time … cycle?' the voice asked. Mrs. Butler recovered from her surprise and tried to explain how we measured minutes, hours, and days. 'What … constitutes … a … day … and … what … constitutes … a … night?' the voice continued. "'A day is approximately twelve hours long—and a night is twelve hours long,' Mrs. Butler replied. There were a few more innocuous questions, and then the other woman came out of her trance." (Keel 1970b, p. 184)

The object flew off. Mrs. Butler wrote to Keel, who interviewed her over the phone. She mentioned strange voices coming over her CB radio, and she was the one to bring up the subject of peculiar visitors, including Major French in May 1967: "'Everything he was wearing was *brand-new*,' she observed. He drove a white mustang, and her husband copied down the license number and had it checked out later. It proved to be a rented car from Minneapolis.

"'He said his stomach was bothering him,' she noted. "I told him that what he needed was some Jell-O. He said if it kept bothering him, he would come back for some.'" (Keel 1970b, page 185)

The next morning French returned. He still complained about his stomach, so there followed the infamous Jell-O drinking bit. "Richard French" visited some friends of the Butlers in Forest City, Iowa, but afterwards vanished forever. Keel has made much of the fact that a genuine Richard French was serving in the Air Force in Minnesota at the time. As Jenny Randles explains: "There was also a Richard French in the USAF, but he denied 'pestering' the Butlers and the USAF proved his case by showing French's identification. The real Richard French bore no resemblance to the man who called at their home." (Randles, p. 99)

Page 20: UFO pilots: The odd-but-still-passable-as-human UFOnauts of the early days have been superseded by "Grays." There are lesser-known types reported, like "Reptoids" and "Nordics," but the Grays hold the majority. This may be partially due to sociological factors. Nearly all popular portraits of extraterrestrials look like Grays, and an old comic book I own (Dell Comics' *Flying Saucers* No. 5, October 1969), which depicts the "Kelly-Hopkinsville" incident and the "Bellicose

Dwarves" of South America, makes the entities involved look very Gray-like.

Page 23: Lieutenant Colonel Maston M. Jacks appears in John G. Fuller's *Incident at Exeter*. Fuller met Jacks in January 1966, at the Pentagon: "I asked him if he would like to review the tape recordings of the people I had interviewed in the Exeter area, but he wasn't interested. 'I told a neighbor of mine, someone who is supposed to have seen one of these things,' he said. 'And I said: If you want to believe in UFOs, have fun. Enjoy it. God bless you.'" (Fuller, pp. 215–216)

CHAPTER THREE

Page 26: *New York Sun* and *New York Times* "batmen": The *Times* article ends with some political sniping and satire, but that doesn't mean the story was imaginary.

Page 27: Winged beings: A short notice appeared in *The Zoologist*, Vol. 26, (July 1868), p. 1295, of a creature seen flying over a mine at Copiapo, Chile, in April of that year. It was observed at about 5 pm one evening. While the workmen were gathering for supper, suddenly a monstrous bird approached, flying from the northwest to the southeast: "As it was passing a short distance above our heads we could mark the strange formation of its body. Its immense wings were clothed with a grayish plumage, its monstrous head was like that of a locust, its eyes were wide open and shone like burning coals; it seemed to be covered with something resembling the thick and stout bristles of a boar ..."

Page 28: Angels without wings: Genesis (19:1–3): "And there came two angels to Sodom at even; and Lot sat in the gate of Sodom: and Lot seeing them rose up to meet them; and he bowed himself with his face toward the ground;

"And he said, Behold now, my lords, turn in, I pray you, into your servant's house, and tarry all night, and wash your feet, and ye shall rise up early, and go on your ways. And they said, Nay; but we will abide in the street all night.

"And he pressed upon them greatly; and they turned in unto him, and entered into his house; and he made them a feast, and did bake unleavened bread, and they did eat."

Thus also the famous warning in "The Epistle of Paul the Apostle to the Hebrews" (13:1–2): "Let brotherly love continue. Be not forgetful to entertain strangers: for thereby some have entertained angels unawares."

Page 28: "…the famous Russian traveler V. K. Arsenyev …" In a different translation, the footprint Arsenyev describes is identified as a bear's, as opposed to the flying creature's.

Paul Stonehill, Director of the Russian Ufology Research Center in California, has kept in close contact with his colleagues in the former Soviet Union. In the early 1990s, he received news about the legendary Letayuschiy Chelovek, the Flying Man of Vladivostok, from Alexander Rempel, a leading ufologist in the far eastern sections of Russia.

Most reports of the Flying Man describe only its strange call, a woman-like scream that ends in a howl. The cry is accompanied by sounds as if something large is approaching through the forest, but nothing is seen. Otherwise fearless hunting dogs flee the creature. The howls of the Flying Man were reported in the 1930s and '40s, and from 1989 on they have been heard again.

Could some more mundane bird be making these noises?

"Yen Vanshen [a witness] is offended. Having spent all his life in the taiga, he knows every bird there is. No, it was the devil, according to the Chinese man." [Stonehill, p. 50]

In recent times, there have been more sightings of the Flying Man. One A. I. Kurentsov, camping near the site of Arsenyev's encounter, awoke in the night with an inexplicable feeling of fear. He rolled onto all fours and checked the large bonfire by which he slept: "Suddenly his lateral vision registered something huge and dark that was swiftly falling onto the bonfire. Falling on his back to eschew any impact, the hunter saw a creature that had a humanoid shape. He discerned webbed, batlike wings. The hunter got up quickly, hid himself behind the trunk of the nearest tree, and did not leave it until daybreak." [Stonehill, p.52]

The reports from eastern Russia stirred a memory of Stonehill's own. Many years ago, his father had been a soldier in the Soviet Army, stationed in the Far East. One day his unit came upon a severely wounded Chinese man lying in the snow and several wolves shot dead around him. He claimed to be a hunter who had been attacked by gold-smugglers, but the unusual make of his pistol convinced the commanding Soviet officer that he was a spy. The man was given some local "moonshine" for his pain, whereupon he told them "to be aware of a 'flying creature, sounding like a human female (zhenschina-samka) in extreme pain.'" [p. 49] The man was left to die, and the men did indeed hear strange noises from the taiga for several nights thereafter.

Ikals: Jacques Vallee, in *Passport to Magonia*, mentions Brian Stross, an American anthropologist working with the Tzeltal Indians of Mexico. After they spotted a strange light in the sky, Stross and his Tzeltal assistant discussed the *ikals*: "The *ikals* are three-foot tall, hairy, black humanoids whom the natives encounter frequently, and Stross learned:

"'About twenty years ago, or less, there were many sightings of this creature or creatures, and several people apparently tried to fight it with machetes. One man also saw a small sphere following him from about five feet. After many attempts he finally hit it with his machete and it disintegrated, leaving only an ash-like substance.'" [Vallee, page 61]

[The *ikals* of the Tzeltals are quite similar to the Proto-Pygmies, the *aluxob* of the Yucatan, which I investigated on site in the 1980s. —Loren.]

Supposedly the *ikals* fly with a "rocket" on their back. They have been known to attack people, paralyze them, and sometimes even carry them off to their cave-lairs.

Page 29: Garuda: Peter Costello points out in his cryptozoological book *The Magic Zoo* that images of Garuda were usually found in temples dedicated to Vishnu: "It seems that the Garuda was an older god than Vishnu, perhaps one of the aboriginal animistic gods which were taken over by the invading Hindus." [Costello, p. 81]

Eventually, humans being what they are, Garuda became less important than Vishnu and ended up as little more than a flying mount. At the same time, he became more manlike. He is usually depicted as having a human body, a beaked, birdlike head, and wings sprouting from his shoulders.

Louisville, Kentucky: Charles Fort writes in *Lo!* (1931): "Louisville *Courier-Journal*, July 29, Aug. 6, 1880 ... The story is that, between 6 and 7 o'clock, evening of July 28th, people in Louisville saw in the sky 'an object like a man, surrounded by machinery, which he seemed to be working with his hands and feet.' The object moved in various directions, ascending and descending, seemingly under control. When darkness came, it disappeared." [Fort, p. 641]

In *Weird America*, Jim Brandon adds that "a tall and thin weirdo" with a metallic helmet and a long cape appeared in the Louisville vicinity that very day: "On his chest under the cape was a large, bright light. His big thing seemed to be scaring people—particularly women—sometimes getting so familiar as to pull their clothing off. His favorite method of escape was by springing smoothly over high objects like haystacks or wagons, then vanishing on the other side." [Brandon, page 92]

In other words, the "weirdo" was England's favorite bogey, Spring-Heeled Jack, down to the last detail. I have not, however, come across any other mention of the Louisville "Jack" appearance.

Page 30: 1946 Batplane: This report comes from Harold T. Wilkins' *Flying Saucers on the Attack*. Miss Young's story was corroborated by a second woman. The "Batplane" was also reported on October 9 over San Diego by a Mr. Mark Probert, a youth named Fernando Esevano, and several others. A "clair-voyant" told Probert the winged vessel was called a *Kareeta*, from "some planet west of the moon." See also the Fortean Society's *Doubt* #17 (1947), p. 251.

Crow: Dr. Harris' letter is reprinted in William Corliss' *Mysterious Universe* (Glen Arm, MD: Sourcebook Project, 1979), p. 165.

Lines of "birds"/Palermo: See Fort's *Book of the Damned*, chapter 16.

Page 31: 1947 wave: As its title suggests, Ted Bloecher's *Report on the UFO Wave of 1947* (Washington: NICAP, 1967) is a book on the subject.

"Mystics and quacks": To read Keel, just about everyone who studies the subject of UFOs is a quack, cultist, amateur, or crack-pot. His statements to this effect should be taken with a grain of salt, though ufology does attract a lot of "fringe" people.

People from space: I heard somewhere that the first person to suggest seriously that flying saucers were spaceships from other worlds was Major Donald E. Keyhoe in his seminal article "Flying Saucers Are Real," in *True* magazine (January 1950), but I can't be sure. Certainly, Charles Fort suggested that we had had visitors from elsewhere, and the concept of alien invaders was popular in science fiction since Wells' *War of the Worlds* (1897).

Flying men: Mrs. Zaikowski [first name actually Bernice]: *Portland* [Oregon] *Journal*, January 21, 1948. Viola Johnson: See *Strange Creatures from Time and Space* (hereafter SCFTAS), p. 207, and Clark and Coleman's article, "Winged Weirdies."

"Kenneth Arnold, who investigated some UFO sightings after his own flying saucer encounter, heard of two more flying men sightings from Butte, Oregon, seen at dawn on September 16, 1948." (Coleman 2002, p. 30)

Ufologist (and movie stuntman) Peter Hassall collected numerous reports of flying men (along with flying platforms and car-like vehicles) in two articles for the *Fortean Times*: "Aeronauts from the Future" (*FT* no. 240, Oct. 2008), and "Motorists from the Future" (*FT* no. 241, Nov. 2008).

Page 32: Clark and Coleman's article is indispensable. Nearly all later publications concerning "winged weirdoes" draws from it, including later books by Clark and Coleman. Vance Randolph mentions some of the same big bird stories in his book *We Always Lie to Strangers* (1951), over two decades earlier.

Page 33: Houston Bat-Man: "1953, June 18/Hilda Walker/118 E. 3d St. William C. Thompson, 'Houston Bat Man,' *Fate* 6 (Oct. 1953): 26–27, quoting *Houston Chronicle* (undated)," according to the *Geo-Bibliography*. Coleman's *Mysterious America* (1983) gives more information.

Ken Gerhard, former Houston resident, attempted to locate the address of the "Bat-Man" sighting but learned that the area had been torn down for the expansion of a highway, Interstate 10. However, he also learned that employees at the Houston Bellaire Theater reportedly saw "a gigantic helmeted man, crouched down and attempting to hide on the roof of a downtown building one night during the 1990s." [Gerhard and Redfern, p. 94] Perhaps the Houston Bat-Man had come back?

Page 34: Winged lady of Vietnam: Witness Earl Morrison is a step-nephew of investigator Don Worley, which is how this case came to light.

Page 38: Loch Ness: Monster-hunter F. W. "Ted" Holiday noted that the lake monsters of Great Britain seemed to avoid cameras deliberately—their presence even making cameras malfunction. As an example, he mentions two women who photographed a pair of monsters at Fort Augustus in 1970: "While they were choosing a suitable background, a large long-necked animal came into view round a headland out in the loch. Presently, it was joined by a similar but smaller creature. Portraits were forgotten as a number of pictures were shot of these creatures until they sank from view ... This film turned out a complete blank. The mechanism had failed to wind the film into frame and the shutter had simply been clicking on a piece of static backing-paper." [Holiday, pp. 191–192]

CHAPTER FOUR

Page 41: Salt Lake City: *Deseret News*, July 18, 1966. See also "Winged Weirdies."

Page 43: "Dinosaur reports." In 1975 a book called *Extraterrestrial Intervention: The Evidence* was published by "Jacques Bergier and the Editors of INFO." On page 105, under the title "Dinosaurs on the Loose Again," there appears the following: "In the summer of 1969 I received a couple of letters passing along rumors that a dinosaur was roaming about Texas. According to one story, said saurian had hauled a car 200 feet off the road and killed its driver. Attempts to track these tales down proved futile, so the Texas dinosaur was entered into our "hearsay" file and forgotten."

This passage supposedly came from *Strange Creatures from Time and Space*—but I've read that book many times, and there's nothing like it in there! In *Fate* magazine, Keel expanded on dinosaurs: "There is a place in Massachusetts where people have been seeing dinosaurs in recent years ... These huge animals seem to melt into nothingness in a small, wooded area. Other events in the same area suggest that some kind of time warp may exist there..." [Keel, March 1991, pp. 22, 26]

As long as we're digressing into modern dinosaurs, here's a strange excerpt by Bob Rickard from *Fortean Times* #40: "The following tantalizing letter appeared in *Empire Magazine* (Denver, Colorado) 22 Aug. 1982, from a Myrtle Snow, of

Pagosa Springs, Colorado, who was convinced she had seen 'five baby dinosaurs' there in May 1935, when she was three years old. Some months later, she says, a farmer, John Martinez, shot one which he claimed had taken some of his sheep. 'My grandfather took us to see it the next morning. It was about seven feet tall, was grey, had a head like a snake, short front legs with claws that resembled chicken feet, large stout back legs and a long tail.'" [Rickard, p. 8]

Ms. Snow also claims to have seen a green "dinosaur" in a cave in 1937, and, decades later, yet another, while driving between Chama, New Mexico and Pagosa Springs (October 23, 1978). Believe it or not, reports of Velociraptor-like "river dinosaurs" have been growing in number in the Colorado area.

Page 46: "Belief is the enemy." Keel has been called "professionally gullible" and "Occam's Magnet," accepting (apparently) almost any weird story and giving a paranormal twist to simple coincidences. Yet his warning against accepting belief-systems is one that all investigators should take to heart.

This is an attitude shared by granddaddy anomalist Charles Fort. "I believe in nothing," he announces in Chapter Three of *Lo!* "I have shut myself away from the rocks and wisdoms of ages, and from the so-called great teachers of all time, and perhaps because of that isolationism I am given to bizarre hospitalities."

But Fort, Keel, and all other human beings tend to speculate. I think that anomalous phenomena may give, let us say, vectors that point toward certain theories—but I doubt we will ever prove these theories beyond the shadow of a doubt. Thus one should never clutch a theory or a doctrine to one's chest and believe in it 100 percent.

By the way, wasn't anyone else annoyed by that poster in Fox Mulder's office that proclaimed, "I WANT TO BELIEVE"?

Page 48: Sistersville Airship: "1897, April 18/[witnessed by] W. E. Roe/*Marietta (O.) Daily Register*, 19 Apr. 1897," according to the *Geo-Bibliography*.

Page 48: "Early in November, an elderly man ..." In Jerome Clark's otherwise impeccable *UFO Encyclopedia*, 2nd Edition, Clark writes that "This story, significant if true, does not appear in the extended and sympathetic treatment Keel accords Derenberger in *The Mothman Prophecies*." (Second Edition, Volume One, p. 329) Obviously it does.

CHAPTER FIVE

Page 52: Quite a few people saw *something* around the time and place Derenberger met Cold, it appears. A Parkersburg businessman named Walter Vanscoy admitted: "I observed a panel truck parked on the berm of the Southbound lanes of I-77 ... I also observed what appeared to be a man standing by the right-hand front door of the panel truck." Several nearby residents told the police of bad TV reception at that time, and a couple of witnesses noted a beam of light in the sky around 7:30 pm. [Clark, pp. 328–329]

Mrs. Frank Huggins: "Irma Hudgins, her son Fred, and her daughter Pamela Sue," according to Clark; their sighting of an identical object was at the same place, at about the same time (6:45 PM), but two days later.

Page 53: "Uninhabited": See also the foldout map "Indians of North America" from *National Geographic*, December 1972.

Curse of Chief Cornstalk: "A rare historical document relates that before he died he put a curse on the town." That's all we learn of the source of the Curse from *The Silver Bridge* (p. 115). In Wamsley's *Mothman: Behind the Red Eyes* (p. 117), a news clipping from 1967 calls the curse a "myth"; it seems one Holly Simmons of the West Virginia State Historical Society discovered there was no truth to the story. But even the news story admitted that many local people had heard of the curse "since early childhood."

Page 54: "Mooneyed people": See James Mooney's *Myths of the Cherokee* pp. 22–23.

"Back hills of Kentucky and Tennessee": The "white Indians" of Kentucky are thought by some to be the descendants of Prince Madoc, the Welsh prince, and his followers, who supposedly sailed to North America in the 12th century. (Brandon, p. 93) Several theories exist to explain the Melungeons of Tennessee, ranging from Madoc's people to a Lost Tribe of Israel. The Melungeons themselves believe that they are descended from Portuguese colonists. (Brandon, pp. 210–211)

Most books on New Jersey mention the "Pineys". They are a poverty-stricken group in the Jersey Pine Barrens, whose origin was probably multi-ethical. See, for instance, McCloy and Miller, pp. 18–20.

[A recent major motion picture, *Out of the Furnace* (2013)—directed by Scott Cooper; produced by Ridley Scott and Leonardo DiCaprio; and starring Woody Harrelson, Christian Bale, Casey Affleck, Willem Dafoe, Zoe Saldana, Forest Whitaker, and Sam Shepard—touches on this theme of similar isolated peoples. They allegedly live in the remote Ramapo Valley, a breathtaking beautiful section of the Ramopo Mountains that crosses the New York/New Jersey border at Suffern, New York. This alleged group of renegade Native Americans, escaped slaves, Hessian mercenary deserters, and West Indian prostitutes living there have come to be known by the derogatory and racist term, the "Jackson Whites." —Loren.]

Page 54: "galaxy of Ganymede": Keel and other writers have harped on the fact that Ganymede is a moon of Jupiter. Cripes, there can be more than one thing named Ganymede in the infinite universe!

"Lanulos": I wonder if there's any significance to the fact that this name is an anagram of "Sol" and "Luna."

Pages 54–55: "Naturally there was no war, poverty, hunger, or misery." Since about 1980 John Keel has denied ever believing in Derenberger's contacts. In *Fate* magazine (April 2002), for instance, he says: "As for Indrid Cold, I never talked to him on the telephone. I always thought Woodrow Derenberger probably made him up." [p. 6] In *The Mothman Prophecies,* I can find only slightly sarcastic lines like the above that suggest he didn't take Woody and Indrid Cold seriously.

Page 55: Gray Barker: The publisher of Saucerian Books, Barker turns out to have been quite a hoaxer. He brought the concept of "Men-in-Black" to prominence by publishing such books as *They Knew Too Much about Flying Saucers* and *Flying Saucers and the Three Men* (the latter by Albert K. Bender). Some investigators have claimed that he actually went "into the field," so to speak, dressed as a Man-in-Black, harassing UFO witnesses on his own time!

A friend of Barker's, John C. Sherwood, wrote an expose about the man, "Gray Barker: My Friend, the Myth-Maker," for *The Skeptical Inquirer* (May/June 1998). It was later published online. Curiously enough, Sherwood gives a sort of backhanded support to the Mothman sequence: "An interim letter, recounting his work on a book about the West Virginia 'Mothman' sightings, reflects Gray's attitude about publishing fiction as nonfiction: 'About half of it is a recounting of actual sightings and events in the Ohio Valley circa 1966.... I think that the "true accounts" are told in an exciting way, but I have deliberately stuck in fictional chapters based roughly on cases I had heard about.'"

What Keel, Sherwood, and others forget is that *Silver Bridge* is admitted to be fictionalized in its own introduction (written by Allen H. Greenfield). Reading it with other Mothman books at hand, it is fairly easy to identify the fictional sections (like the personal adventures of Indrid Cold and the Men in Black), while it expands on known accounts of the flying entity (Bandit the German Shepherd, for instance, and the Scarberrys' and Mallettes' long night of fleeing Mothman).

Some of Barker's attitude leaks through the pages of his book *The Silver Bridge*. After mentioning the Men-in Black, he writes: "No doubt many UFO enthusiasts, reading of the men in black, picked up their telephones and rang up people who they knew were frightened by the idea, and spoke dire warnings to them in assumed foreign accents, usually German." [Barker, page 91]

Bandit, the German Shepherd: The biggest news in Jeff Wamsley's *Mothman: Behind the Red Eyes* is probably the revelations about the Bandit incident. First of all, the primary witness' name is Merle, not Newell Partridge, as has been given in every Mothman book, magazine article, and contemporary news clipping. (He must have answered to "Newell" occasionally, as the mistake was even on his birth certificate.)

Page 56: Salem, West Virginia: We've just heard about Salem, Oregon. The Name Game at work? In Wamsley's book, Partridge says he lived closer to Center Point, WV.

Page 56: Keel uses Barker's tape-recorded interview with Partridge here. In Wamsley (p. 50), Partridge reports that the picture tube exploded, sending debris across the room. A neighbor who lived two miles away reported his TV also exploded, at about the same time.

Barker was not the only person to interview Merle Partridge. The witness told Jeff Wamsley that "an Air Force colonel, a detective, and a few others" visited him the day after he reported Bandit missing (Wamsley, p. 48).

[At the Mothman Festival in 2016 in Point Pleasant, my wife Jenny and I were startled to have Roger, the grown son of the late Merle/Newell Partridge, quietly introduce himself to us. He was the actual owner of Bandit, whom he loved dearly as his pet. —Loren]

Red eyes: Partridge now reveals that what he (and his wife) saw were two red lights, "going in circles." He denies seeing red "eyes." The next morning, he found a circle of pressed-down grass 40-to-50-feet wide—making this event an "ordinary" UFO landing rather than a Mothman sighting. (Too bad—the image of Mothman at the far end of a field, perhaps near a hay barn, has been an archetypical image to me since 1970, and that was inspired by the Bandit incident.)

Page 57: Bandit vanishing: It would not have been too easy to just carry off this dog, according to Partridge: "I don't know of any animal capable of killing that dog, because I know I have tried to hold his head between my hands; and Roger, my oldest boy, and I, have both tried to hold that dog on the ground while playing with him, and both of us together couldn't hold him down." [Barker, p. 26]

Other strange things happened near Partridge's home and to the man himself. For a week or so after the dog's disappearance, silence reigned throughout the countryside. "You didn't hear a cricket … you didn't hear a bird … you didn't hear a cow moo." (Wamsley, p. 51) Two weeks later a neighbor was forced off the road by "something" with flashing lights, and the man's youngest son vanished from his car. Partridge helped search for the boy, who reappeared walking up the road from the opposite direction of his father's route of travel. Even decades later, the boy could not say what happened during his "missing time."

Odd events seemed to follow Partridge for years when he drove trailer trucks, ranging from a "bluish glow" that shorted out the battery and electronic gear to awakening from a nap to find the cab—and himself—covered with spider webs!

Page 57: Just to be complete, "Mineralwells" is a single word.

CHAPTER SIX

For those of you who own *Mothman: The Facts Behind the Legend*, the following list might be helpful in the Eyewitness Reports section:

Eyewitness #1 = Mary Mallette
Eyewitness #2 = Roger Scarberry
Eyewitness #3 = Steve Mallette
Eyewitness #4 = Gary Northrup
Eyewitness #5 = Deputy Millard Halstead
Eyewitness #6 = Ralph or (more likely) Virginia Thomas

Page 58: Before that fateful November 15, rumors already made the rounds of something strange in West Virginia. On Saturday, November 12, Kenneth Duncan of Blue Creek was digging a grave for his late father-in-law, Homer Smith, near Clendenin. Four other men—Bob Lovejoy, Bill Poole, Andrew Godby, and Emil Gibson—were helping him. Suddenly something that "looked like a brown human being" came gliding between the trees of the rural gravesite, "in sight for about a minute." (Keel 1968; newspaper clippings in Wamsley, pp. 51 and 99)

A year or so earlier, a seven-year-old boy ran into his house and told his mother that he had seen "an angel ... a man with wings." The woman, who lived a few miles from Clendenin, was amused at her son's imagination. In the summer of 1966, another woman, out in her backyard, was stunned to see something like "a giant butterfly" soar past. (Keel 1970a, p. 213)

Page 59: Generator plant: The North Power Plant was torn down *ca.* 1993.

November 15, 1966: Night of the Leonid meteor shower, this night's being one of the brightest meteor showers on record. Coincidence?

Page 60: "It turned slowly": Linda Scarberry, in Sergent/ Wamsley, states that Mothman had a wing caught in a guide wire near the power plant. She also says it had humanlike arms as well as legs; "Its hands were really big." [p. 20] This is the first time, to my knowledge, Mothman was described with arms. *Strange Creatures* states flatly "No witness has ever reported seeing arms." [p. 229]

[Scarberry's early story of no arms, no hands grew compromised and was elaborated down through the years. By the time the Sergent/Wamsley book appeared, her sighting was being told differently than it originally had been. —Loren.]

Page 60: Dead dog: Barely mentioned here or in *SCFTAS*, the dead dog (Bandit?) by the road sequence is quite bizarre in Barker's *Silver Bridge*. After discussing their sighting at Dairyland, the young quartet decided to drive out to the TNT Area again. Once they neared the farm of C. C. Lewis, however, they began to chicken out. At the "Lewis Gate"—a popular landmark, being the only place for miles one could turn around easily—Roger pulled in to turn. The headlights flashed over the dog:

"'Get out, Steve,' Mary begged, 'and see if it's hurt badly. Maybe we can take it to a veterinary.'

"'It's dead, I can tell,' Steve said as he shined the light on it again; 'dead as a doornail.'

"'Then, from behind a tree, or from the ditch,' Roger told us, 'this thing came out and jumped over the car.'" [Barker, p. 43]

The scribbled notes by Linda, Roger, and Mary agree with Barker's account of the dog-by-the-road incident. At this point the frightened quartet visited Tiny's Restaurant to get owner Gary Northrup's advice. Seeing how genuinely frightened the teens were, Northrup called the police.

The implication is strong that the dead dog, instead of being Mothman's dinner, was bait to get someone to stop and possibly leave their car. Why? Perhaps it's better not to know. Was it coincidence that it was the same carload of kids who fell for the dead dog trick? That question cannot be answered.

[Remember that the *Silver Bridge* is fiction. We are unsure how much Gray Barker made up, for novelistic effect. —Loren.]

Page 61: Going back to the power plant: Linda Scarberry's scribbled notes from 1966 state she saw Mothman out in a pasture but walking towards the [presumably moving] car as they led Deputy Halstead to the TNT Area. [Sergent/Wamsley p. 43] Mary and Roger's notes agree with this. All three contemporary accounts mention a cloud of "dust or smoke" rising from the coal yard near the plant.

Only a few days after the November 15 car chase, two teenage boys, Bob Bosworth and Alan Coates, entered the North Power Plant at night and had a creepy encounter with a silent, hulking *something* on the third floor of the dilapidated factory. See Wamsley, pp. 17–28.

The name Mothman: A news clipping in Sergent/Wamsley, undated but written no later than the Thursday or Friday after the Tuesday encounter, is headlined MASON COUNTIANS HUNT 'MOTH MAN,' so someone named the creature very quickly.

A *Point Pleasant Register* editorial written by John Samsell (Thursday, Nov. 17), mentions that newscasters elsewhere in the country were calling the thing a "monster moth," "red-eyed demon," or "bird man." (Sergent/Wamsley, p. 71) I've always gotten the impression John Keel disliked the name Mothman, as he usually refers to it simply as "the Bird."

[The generally agreed upon reality is that a copyeditor at the *Athens Messenger*, a fan of the popular *Batman* television series (1966–1968), created the "Moth Man," then "Mothman" moniker via the headlines of that paper. —Loren.]

Page 62: trigger-happy hero: "One officer heard an automatic rifle bark several times Thursday night behind one of the many buildings," according to an *Athens Messenger* story by Roger Bennett (Nov. 18, 1966).

Page 63: Wamsley/Thomas sighting: In her interview with Jeff Wamsley, Marcella Bennett says that her brother Raymond was trying to get her to look at some strange lights in the sky as they were leaving the Thomas house, lights bright enough to hurt one's eyes. Moments later Mothman held everyone's attention. In *Strange Creatures,* Mrs. Bennett was left to pull herself together, pick up her daughter, and then make for the house. Five years later Raymond Wamsley more-or-less pulls her from the clutches of Mothman. An attempt by a male ego to save face in the later version, or was it a correction? It is a very human touch to a weird tale.

A clipping from the *Athens Messenger,* undated but presumably around Nov. 17, states: "Later they ventured outside and spotted the creature watching them while partially hidden behind a pile of bricks." [Sergent and Wamsley, p. 86] It then flew away. This seems to verify the implication that Mothman "haunted" certain people, observing them (and vice-versa) multiple times.

Although Mrs. Bennett never encountered Men-in-Black (surely the Fright-Wig Man was bad enough), her collection of Mothman and UFO clippings disappeared from her house while she was on a trip to Columbus, Ohio. This was about a year after the sightings died down. (Wamsley, p. 77)

An article from the *Columbus Dispatch* (Friday, Nov. 18) states that on this same Wednesday night an anonymous Cheshire, Ohio, man claimed that the winged creature chased him near Gallipolis, Ohio.

Page 68: In interviews (*The Search for the Mothman* documentary, *Unsolved Mysteries'* "Mothman" segment, and Wamsley's *Mothman: Behind the Red Eyes*), Thomas Ury has maintained that the thing he saw was definitely a bird—a frighteningly huge and strange looking avian, but a bird nonetheless.

Never interviewed by Keel or Gray Barker, Ury had only a few quibbles with the account printed in the local newspapers by Mary Hyre. His bird did not lift straight up like a helicopter but rose smoothly above the tree line like one. It did not appear from the direction of the TNT Area but rose from the bank of the Ohio River and returned there. Ury does admit that he never saw its wings flap, and that it was incredibly fast, literally flying circles around his car even as he reached 90 miles an hour.

Like other witnesses, he could not describe the creature in detail. It was covered with very ruffled feathers, and it was "a brownish, grayish, blackish, ugly looking thing." (Wamsley, p. 102)

In one of those curious coincidences that surround Fortean flaps, Ury learned years later that Gray Barker's office was located directly above the shoe store where Ury worked! When Ury complained about the inaccuracies of Barker's *Silver Bridge*, Barker chalked them up to "poetic license." (Wamsley, p. 98)

Though Ury himself had no further trouble, his mother claimed to receive strange phone calls in the middle of the night. If she answered, all she would hear were beeps like Morse code. Also, her lights would go out while the houses around her stayed lit. She did not tell her son of her experiences until about a year before the Wamsley interview.

One more odd detail: Mrs. Hyre's newspaper story suggests that the giant bird came from behind Homer Smith's house. Ury has corrected this mistake, but the late Homer Smith managed to get mentioned in the Mothman saga again (see notes for page 58).

Page 72: 14-foot monster traps. Yes, I admit it, as a naive youth I thought he really had monster traps, and I whiled away a few afternoons wondering if they were 14-foot tall traps, or if they were for 14-foot tall monsters.

"I know from bitter experience that some of my humorous comments will be taken seriously and will prompt new venom," says Keel in *Our Haunted Planet* (pp. 9–10).

CHAPTER SEVEN

Page 77: Eddy Adkin's bird: This account stands out because the enormous bird at the Gallipolis airport is said to have an extremely long neck, while Mothman seemed to have little or no neck (some even described it as headless, the red eyes set directly on the body). I have noticed myself that cranes and other birds can fold up their necks and long-billed heads as they soar, giving the impression of a headless gliding form.

Page 79: Visiting the TNT area: The witnesses' handwritten notes from 1966 describe their own return to the power plant the Wednesday and Thursday after the Tuesday night misadventure. On Wednesday, the original witnesses (and a few other people) discovered strange footprints near the North Power Plant, like two horseshoes stuck side by side. They entered the building, and soon Steve Mallette fled, claiming to have seen "the red eyes" inside a huge boiler. On Thursday, the witnesses were accompanied by several reporters. They heard a loud clanging noise inside the power plant and found that one of the boiler doors that they had closed only minutes before was open again. Thursday evening Linda Scarberry and Mary Hyre supposedly saw "the red eyes" in a fenced-off field near the plant.

Page 80: Deputy Alva Sullivan: The Name Game? Keel's first name was originally Alva. Well, how many Alvas do you know?

Page 82: Zone of fear: Unreasoning fear in forests and other desolate places seems to be a phenomenon in and of itself, believed in ancient Greece to have been caused by the pipes of Pan, the God of Nature (literally, "panic"). Some paranormal beings seem to give off such an aura to this day, as in tales of the Scottish entity known as the Gray Man of Ben MacDhui.

An Aside: The Bull in the Field
The blurb on the back of *The Mothman Prophecies* calls it "A True Story of Unexplained Terror." Perhaps this is why Keel fails to mention Woodrow Derenberger's bull.

In *SCFTAS*, Keel explains that he and Gray Barker traveled together to Mineralwells to meet Derenberger for the first time.

After interviewing the contactee, the investigators spotted small bobbing lights in a field behind the Derenberger residence. Naturally, they marched off into the night for a closer look. Derenberger neglected to tell them that an angry bull dwelt in the field ... or that the area was bounded by an electric fence.

Barker remembered the incident well: "John reached it [the fence] first and started to throw his long legs over it. Suddenly he let out a yelp and sailed over the fence, sprawling headlong in a big mud puddle on the other side." (Barker, p. 70)

Barker was not inclined to follow. Keel climbed a wooded hill, and eventually Derenberger ambled out to join Barker.

"He shouldn't go up there alone. There's a bull in that field," the contactee said unhelpfully.

Fortunately, Keel knew that the worse thing one can do is run from a bull. He flashed his light in its eyes and walked boldly past it rather than away from it. He concluded that the bobbing lights were car headlights on the far side of the valley, flickering between the trees on the hilltop. (Keel 1970a, p. 179)

CHAPTER EIGHT

Page 86: "The strange ones..." In an interview with Doug Skinner for the *Fortean Times*, Keel says he looked for but could not find cult activity in the Point Pleasant area. Donnie Sergent, on the other hand, in his interview with Linda Scarberry, said he had heard about "Satanic rituals" in the TNT area. Linda replied: "We saw those people up there a couple of times. They always scattered when we came back by for the second time. They had a cross up on a tree out there one night when we drove by." [Sergent and Wamsley, p. 23]

Page 87: Marcella Bennett's Mothman sighting is mentioned in *SCFTAS* without the later assault by the "Fright-Wig Man." The Tor paperback *The Mothman Prophecies* does not carry the Afterword from the 1991 IlliumiNet edition, where Keel enlarges upon the man in the Ford Galaxy: "The man in the fright wig who molested many women in the Point Pleasant area was never identified or captured. I always felt that he was really the key figure in the whole situation and may have been linked to the mutilated (sacrificed?) dogs and other animals." [pp. 273–274]

Page 88: Mrs. Hyre's strange visitor: It is curious that the MIB and other oddballs who show up in paranormal hotspots sometimes display supernormal knowledge, yet at other times seem lost, confused, and rather dim-witted. Some are certainly human enough, hoaxers or just plain strange people attracted to such events. Others act like badly-programmed androids. Some act normal but finally reveal a bizarre quirk, as with "Richard French."

Page 89+: "Tiny" and other MIB: Perhaps these people carry some sort of anti-gravity apparatus. Shuttle astronaut William Pogue explains the effects of zero-g on the body in his book *How Do You Go to the Bathroom in Space?* One gains an inch or more in height, due to the spine straightening. The body's organs shift upward, giving one a "wasp waist." The movement of internal organs also means that one cannot inhale deeply (as with those MIB who wheeze?). Most interesting of all: "Loose flesh on the face rises, or floats, on the bone structure, giving a high-cheek-boned or 'Oriental' appearance." (Pogue, p. 10)

Page 95: Tall figure in white cape: Reminiscent of England's Spring-Heeled Jack.

Page 97: Warning to Tad Jones: Keel leaves off the final line, "You want be warned again," found in *SCFTAS*. See the "there want [*sic*] be another warning" farther down the page. Good spelling is wanting among the MIB.

Page 98: Strange footprints: The footprints found by Linda Scarberry and company near the generator plant and the Thomas house resembled small "double hoofprints." Footprints that appear from nowhere and end abruptly are common in "hairy humanoid" reports. Giant dog tracks and naked human print: a werewolf? When I first wrote that comment, I was being facetious. In recent years, however, reports of werewolf-like creatures have had a major upswing. See Linda Godfrey's books *The Beast of Bray Road* (2003) and *Hunting the American Werewolf* (2006).

Page 101: CIA paranoia: Keel's Asia trip was documented in his first book, *Jadoo* (1957).

Page 102: Watergate, Kennedy assassination: A big can of worms that I'd rather not open. An odd fellow who was a player in the "Dero" tales of Richard Shaver, the early flying saucer/MIB case of Maury Island, and the Kennedy assassination was Fred Crisman. See Kenn Thomas' *Maury Island UFO: The Crisman Conspiracy* (San Francisco: Last Gasp of San Francisco, 1999).

CHAPTER NINE

Pages 103–104: Blue Fireball: A curious encounter that brings in the attraction of "phenomena" to lovers and Lovers' Lanes, missing time, nighttime "sunburns," and other details that are cliché in UFO stories now but were new in 1966 (even in 1975, when *Mothman* was published).

Page 105: "...programmed to love ..." In the opinions of medieval scholars, incubi and succubi—the sex-oriented demons who had intercourse with mortals—were not beings of flesh, therefore incubi could not produce sperm. The theory was that a succubus received a man's semen, transformed into an incubus, and then impregnated a woman. Is this all a eugenics program by unknown intelligences? Merlin from Arthurian legend was supposedly the product of such a demonic union.

Pages 105–107: Don Estrella: This UN representative appears to have been cursed like others in the Mothman saga. He returned to his native Portugal and ran a cafe, according to John Keel in a *Fortean Times* interview. "It went broke or something, and he came back to the States. And then he had a terrible accident." (Skinner, p. 34) Keel believes he ended up in a wheelchair.

Page 107: The Grinning Man: Gets a chapter to himself in *SCFTAS*. Particularly eerie is the manifestation at Elizabeth, New Jersey, on October 11, 1966.

Phone Phreaks: Bear in mind that Gray Barker is one of them. In an interview with Jim Keith (August 23, 1996), Keel says: "I raised hell with the phone company, and they tracked down some of the calls I got, and some of them were from Gray Barker." (Keith, p. 158)

Page 108: Numbered People: Perhaps "The Village," from the old British show *The Prisoner*, operates worldwide now. The movie *The Mothman Prophecies* features the enigmatic phrase, "Wake up, Number 37!"

Page 109: UFOs using post-hypnotic suggestion: The beeping noises often described put witnesses into a trance and then bring them out again—but that implies that the people were hypnotized at some point *before* ever encountering funny lights or shiny objects.

Page 110: Kenneth Arnold and Maury Island: Peculiar things certainly happened to Arnold, but the Maury Island sequence was undoubtedly a hoax. ("But whose?", to paraphrase Keel.) Look for Edward J. Ruppelt's 1956 book (old but still one of the best, available from Cosimo Classics): *The Report on Unidentified Flying Objects*. There's also Arnold's own account in *The Coming of the Saucers* (1952), and "The Maury Island Episode" in Curtis Fuller (editor), *Proceedings of the First International UFO Congress*, 1980.

Sonny DesVergers: His controversial claim is usually called "the Florida Scoutmaster case" in UFO literature.

Page 111+: Woody Derenberger is described sympathetically concerning his supposed harassments. But:

Page 112: "Woodrow Derenberger's story troubled me from the outset, and for many reasons."

Page 113: "There was something mundane about Woody's descriptions of that nudist colony in outer space. Too mundane."
More hints that Keel didn't think that much about Derenberger.

Pages 113–114: Jim and Darla: Bear in mind these are two of Woody's friends, who later meet Indrid Cold and company in this "silly episode."

Animal mutilations: Another can of worms! Some books on the subject are *Mystery Stalks the Prairie* (1976) by Keith Wolverton and Roberta Donovan; *Mute Evidence* (1983) by Daniel Kagan and Ian Summers (a skeptical look); Linda Howe's *Alien Harvest* (1988) and *Glimpses of Other Realities* (1994); and Christopher O'Brien's *The Mysterious Valley* (1996).

Page 115: Vampires: Keel has suggested elsewhere that the vampire and werewolf attacks of earlier centuries were folkloric interpretations of the mutilation phenomenon. Charles Fort has similar ideas in *Lo!*

Page 116: Magic ritual: UFOs are "science-fictional" (for lack of a better term); even forces that use blood and flesh to create temporary physical beings could be made to sound scientific. But Keel mixes in black magic, witchcraft, and secret rituals! Our sense of division between the scientific, the psychic, and the supernatural becomes blurred in this world of anomalies and unknown forces.

"... a purpose that might turn our hair gray instantly." Keel and other Fortean writers such as Janet and Colin Bord have suggested that Big Hairy Monsters, phantom panthers, and similar entities are only temporarily "real." After mentioning the propensity for monsters and UFOs to snatch animals and take blood in *SCFTAS*, Keel quotes Jacques Vallee: "The devil does not have a body. Then, how does he manage to have intercourse with men and women? ... All the theologians answer that the devil borrows the corpse of a human being, either male or female, or else he forms with other materials a new body for this purpose." (Vallee, p. 126)

The implication seemed to me to be that some Intelligence somewhere used these stolen biological materials to create chimerical life-forms. Mothmen? Bigfoot-type humanoids? Beings that might even pass themselves off as people? A heady concept for my eleven-year-old self, when I first read *SCFTAS*. "Gross! Cool!" I yelled almost simultaneously.

Page 117: Bloodmobile incident. This is, indeed, an astonishing account. Has anyone ever hunted down Beau Shertzer and/or the nurse for an interview? In the *Search for the Mothman* documentary, the UFO is replaced by the winged apparition in the recreation of this event.

Page 119: Phantasmagoria of UFO sightings. By now even "beings" emerging from a landed saucer and leaving in an ordinary car seem almost acceptable.

Letart Falls angel: The witness is described as a friend of Ben Franklin IV, Gray Barker's traveling companion when the many taped interviews were made. Sidereal phenomena reportedly haunted the witness' family afterwards. Telephones rang with no one there, or ceased functioning entirely. Their TV developed interference, and once "a Communist program" appeared on a supposedly unused channel. (Barker, p. 111)

CHAPTER TEN

Page 122: James Moseley: A fellow who had his finger on the pulse of Ufology (and "Ufoology," as he calls it) for over half a century. In his memoirs, *Shockingly Close to the Truth*, he admits to many a hoax, but even he concedes there is a residue of the truly unknown in UFO lore. *Saucer News* is gone, and so is Moseley and his beloved *Saucer Smear*.

Gray Barker claimed to have questioned Keel straight out on his "mysterious knowledge": "I somehow feel you have theories or some information you're holding out on all of us." There follows a fairly accurate outline of Keel's Ultraterrestrial hypothesis (in *The Silver Bridge*, p. 73).

Page 125: Baby crying: A noise that, along with a sound "like a woman screaming," figures in many ghost and monster stories, especially those featured in *SCFTAS*.

Linda Lilly's intruder: Not only a phantom with a checkered shirt, but also a Grinning Man (see page 107).

Page 126+ : Keel did spend a lot of time with Mary Hyre during this period. No wonder there were rumors. "John Klein's" unfortunate wife is named Mary in *The Mothman Prophecies* movie.

Page 127: UFO disguised as airplane: Seems like this tactic would be a way to fool all those silly earth-people, but these objects frequently do something odd to give themselves away. Mysterious (usually black) helicopters are now a solid part of the "cattle mutilation" mythos.

Page 128: An article by Keel in *Saga's UFO Report*, "Mysterious Voices from Outer Space," expands on the fireball-hitting-the-transmitter incident and other occurrences mentioned in this chapter.

Page 129: Radio static: "He tried switching to several of the 26 available channels but none of them were working. (Later I learned that police and CB radios all up and down the Ohio valley were equally useless that same night.)" (Keel 1975, p. 37.)

Page 130: Purple Blobs: An interesting new phenomenon or creature, assuming they weren't afterimages of some kind. They would be easily overlooked by most people at night. In *Operation Trojan Horse* (pp. 610–611) we are told that "purple blobs" were reported often in the early days of the flying saucer era (seen, for instance, in Seattle, Washington, on June 24, 1947—the date of Kenneth Arnold's seminal saucer sighting). Unfortunately, no sources are given.

Page 132: Thing in the gully: Keel is quite candid in the *Saga* article: "That's right, folks. The fearless world traveler and UFO chaser was scared out of his wits!"

Page 133: This is one of the strangest statements in *The Mothman Prophecies*, that the more-or-less full moon rose one night, failed to appear at all the next (despite the sky being cloudless), then rose as usual the third night. Since Keel mentions lacunal amnesia several times subsequently, perhaps he suffered from "specific forgetting" himself and just didn't enter the moonrise into his memory. Or, taking note of the date, maybe this is an "April Fool's" from him. The "Mysterious Voices" article does not mention the missing moon.

Page 134: False stars: another good way for UFOs to camouflage themselves—but why did they want to hang stark still over these particular hills for nights on end?

For some reason, I was more skeptical of the "false stars" than of other, more spectacular UFO reports. They might pass themselves off as stars to the people directly below, but observers miles away, watching at an angle against clouds and mountains, should know they weren't stars. They would also be able to see them for hours. Why no reports of that?

Other writers have come across the fake stars, however. Possibly the most carefully-prepared, scientifically-oriented attempt to study UFOs was organized in 1973 by Dr. Harley D. Rutledge, a physics professor from the University of Missouri and one-time President of the Missouri Academy of Science, as documented in his book *Project Identification*. The explanations of diffraction images, Questar telescopes, angular resolution, FAA regulations, and ASA film ratings take up more space in the book than UFO hunting, but when Rutledge's group did spot anomalous lights, many of them were what Rutledge calls "pseudostars."

Despite the group's determination to remain strictly scientific in its study of UFOs in and around Piedmont, Missouri, they could not avoid Keelian weirdness. The book dust jacket of *Project Identification* puts it best: "Some objects appeared to mimic the appearance of known aircraft; others flagrantly violated the laws of physics. But most unsettling of all were the lights that repeatedly seemed to react to the project members observing them."

Page 135: Lacunal amnesia: If you lose your memory of certain moments or events these days, more than likely people will conclude you've been abducted and subjected to alien anal probes and whatnot. But here we see the phenomenon occurring to a woman at home with her family.

Page 136: Mrs. Bryant: Her close encounter seems to have happened on the same day as Woodrow Derenberger's (see page 159).

Page 138: Mrs. Bryant is unique to my knowledge in catching her cattle mutilators "red-handed" more than once. Most "mutes" are simply discovered after the fact.

CHAPTER ELEVEN

Pages 140–141: It's truly astonishing that such displays could be witnessed by so many people and simply not affect the rest of the world. Other such mass observations have been reported, however. Dr. Rutledge's group (and dozens of witnesses from all over southeast Missouri) had no trouble finding strange lights in the sky over a period of months in the area around Piedmont, Missouri. (Rutledge, 1973)

Page 144: The Wednesday Phenomenon: There seems to be only one way to determine whether or not there is something to the Wednesday Phenomenon. Someday I'm going through the *Geo-Bibliography of Anomalies* page by page and chart what day every UFO sighting took place on (excluding "Hoaxes" and "?" and other indeterminable details). I shall begin when I have a lot of time on my hands.

Page 145: "Federal Officers": Not Men-in-Black, but FBI agents, apparently.

Page 146: Mary Hyre's affidavit: Although it's nice to know such a document exists, it will prove nothing to most people. There were affidavits for the "David Lang" disappearance and the "Alexander Hamilton" Airship cow-napping, both of which are now known to be hoaxes.

Page 149: In *Fate* magazine (December 1995), Keel expands on Mr. Elmore's encounter. He asked the old fellow to draw the "shed," and Elmore came up with a bizarre conglomeration of cubes and corners standing on metallic legs. Two years later, Keel watched Neil Armstrong and Buzz Aldrin land on the moon in their Lunar Excursion Module (LEM) "Eagle": "A shudder went through me as I watched this historic moment on black-and-white TV along with the rest of the world. Leonard Elmore had been trying to describe a LEM to me!" (Keel 1995, p.26)

Keel then calls to mind the "soda-pop factor," a phrase coined by Dr. James MacDonald after hearing of a contactee whose alien friends landed and asked for bottles of soda pop. In Keel's view the entities do this to make UFO witnesses look "downright silly."

The Mothman Prophecies contains other examples of devices seen before they existed, like the "secret helicopter" of Ohio [page 102].

Page 150: The fake census takers have been replaced with bogus social workers intent on removing children from their homes. Of course, these cases have been dismissed as urban legends—or have they?

"Children vanish more frequently than any other group. We're not talking about ordinary runaways." So says Keel in *Our Haunted Planet* [p. 202].

Certainly the missing children problem is growing at an alarming rate: "The best estimates are that about a million American youngsters leave home each year, with 90 percent returning in two weeks," writes Gary Turbak. "Approximately 100,000 children are thus unaccounted for." This is not even counting the "25,000 to 100,000 stolen by divorced or separated parents." [Turbak, p. 61]

CHAPTER TWELVE

Page 151: Credulity askew: Keel admits that he was sucked into the same mind-games tormenting the oddest of the contactees.

Page 153: Farmer with shotgun: Like the "Beelzebub" opening, this was recreated in the movie. The parallels with the book become more numerous in the movie from here on.

Page 154: Red and white thing: Perhaps this is what took Bandit.

Page 155: "So I would talk to him." Maybe "Tiny" the MIB wore too-short trousers so the wire in his leg would be seen. Also, why was he even wearing the conspicuous badge that he made pains to hide?

Page 157: Knows more contactees than anyone else: Daniel Cohen, author of many non-fiction books for young adults, is skeptical of paranormal phenomena and does not think much of Keel's theories. Still, as he writes in *Voodoo, Devils, and the New Invisible World*: "I can vouch for the fact that he did not just sit back and make up his stories about 'silent contactees' ... I personally have no doubt that today there are tens of thousands of people walking around the streets of America who think that they have talked to people from outer space." (Cohen 1972, p. 134)

Page 158: Mercury, Earth, and Mars: What happened to Venus? Must be some Immanuel Velikovsky thing. Certainly extrasolar planets are being discovered now.

Page 159: Kronin: I get a kick out of the idea that the entities once known as Greek gods may still be manifesting themselves with a change of costume, so to speak.

Mr. Cold: Note that Keel took Derenberger seriously because of the other UFO encounters reported the night he met Indrid Cold.

Page 162: Identical messages: Perhaps people simply deliver "revelations" in similar terms due to the construction of language.

Page 163: Cracked record: This sounds a bit like the "mechanistic supernatural" of H. P. Lovecraft and Charles Fort—only the "mechanism" is broken.

Pages 163–168: A discourse in theories: I carried three major ideas from John Keel's works:

1. The Window Theory, mainly from *SCFTAS*. Essentially, ghosts, UFOs, monsters, and assorted Fortean phenomena appear and disappear in the same distinct areas year after year, even century after century. Keel dubbed these areas "Windows," and in these places it is as if an opening sometimes appears between our earth and some other universe or dimension.

"Some specialists ... have considered ideas involving 'interpenetration.' They speculate that another world exists outside our space-time continuum and that these myriad objects and creatures have found doors from their world to ours in these 'window' sectors." (Keel 1970a, p. 16)

This was my favorite Fortean idea at age 11. It certainly gave one an easy out if an unlikely creature was reported. Where did it come from? Another dimension. Why can't the search parties find it? It went back.

Unfortunately, though Keel kept the "window areas," he dropped the idea of other dimensions as worlds like our own with their own physical inhabitants. Instead he came up with:

2. The Ultraterrestrial Theory. The chapter "Mimics of Man," in *Our Haunted Planet*, outlines the simpler version of the UT theory quite well. Alex Saunders, in *Quest* magazine (October 1969), put it even more succinctly: "Living among us undetected may be creatures (not necessarily alien) with all the outward appearances of human beings." (Keel 1971, pp. 90–91, quoting Saunders)

Other names for these co-inhabitants of our world are: parahumans, mimics, meta-terrestrials, elementals, and OINTs (Ivan Sanderson's acronym for Other Intelligences).

Operation Trojan Horse suggested that there might be several varieties of UTs, ranging from the human looking to the very inhuman. Some might be physical entities, while others might be normally invisible and/or intangible.

I liked this theory, too. There have been plenty of reports of humanoids and phantoms that have nothing to do with UFOs, and of "vehicles" that simply do not seem like spaceships (like the nineteenth century airships and Tad Jones' sphere-with-propeller). Keel, however, could not leave well enough alone, and the UT theory quickly mutated into:

3. The Superspectrum Theory. Pages 163–168 of *The Mothman Prophecies* outline the Superspectrum Theory: that the entire electromagnetic spectrum (including the energies that make telepathy, precognition, and other psychic powers possible) is a single intelligent being, essentially God. History's angels, demons, Greek gods, UFO aliens, and other entities are not individual creatures but temporary "clots" of energy, programmed to perform certain tasks and eventually dissolving back into the Superspectrum. (This is why MIBs act so strangely when faced with something not in their programming, like Jell-O.)

One wonders why the Superspectrum does what it does, and why some of its interventions in human affairs are helpful, but so many others disastrous.

I might suggest a theory combining #2 and #3, that UTs are the imitative force creating false prophets and illuminations, the demons to the Superspectrum's God.

A throwaway line in Chapter Two of *Our Haunted Planet* suggests that UTs are part of the human psyche. Perhaps the Jungian Collective Unconscious is trying to communicate with its individual parts, as a single human's unconscious mind speaks through symbol-laden dreams. The Collective Unconscious' dreams, however, may become visible and solid, possessed of powers we would call magic—as long as the dream lasts.

I could also state that dreams sometimes produce random scenarios, simple repetitions of recent memories, drug- and illness-induced nightmares, and other images that are not related to communication. No wonder we never understand the strange co-inhabitants of this cosmic mud ball.

Page 170: Vanishing houses: Parapsychologists would call these stories of retrocognition, or place memories, recordings of the past somehow impressed on the very environment.

Excalibur: "A Glimpse of Avalon?" from the *London Daily Mirror*, 10 November 1969. Reprinted in *Phenomena: A Book of Wonders* by John Michell and Robert J. M. Rickard (1977).

Rex Ball: A quick googling tells us that Rex Ball's adventure was published in *Document 96—A Rationale for Flying Saucers* by Frank Martin Chase (Gray Barker Books, 1968). Ball was in Illinois at the time, not Georgia.

CHAPTER THIRTEEN

Page 173: "Neurots": They're all online now.

Page 174: Someone must have ordered everyone to shut up: Perhaps this partly explains Keel's phrase "folklore in the making" rumors and false stories intertwining with real reports.

Page 175: So some of the witnesses' names have been altered. Which ones?

Page 175+: Photographers: I once worked with people in charge of foreclosures at the Bank of Oklahoma. Their files were full of photographs of houses from which the unfortunate residents were to be evicted. I noticed that all the pictures had been taken on the move, so to speak, from inside automobiles. Maybe some of these phantom photographers come from financial institutions.

Flash gun: Jim Keith, in his book on MIBs, mentions a secret government "light weapon" meant to temporarily blind the enemy. I suspect this concept eventually became the memory-erasing "flashy-thingy" from Will Smith's *Men in Black* movies.

Page 178: Another mention of unreasoning fear.

Page 179: I've had dreams of a giant eye in the sky, myself.

F. W. Holiday mentions UFOs that look like eyes in Chapter Nine of *The Dragon and the Disk*. He seemed to believe such objects were seen in ancient times and recorded on figurines, pottery, and in mounds. He dubbed the flying ocular organ the "Eye of Odin."

CHAPTER FOURTEEN

Pages 183–184: A classic abduction scenario, though Keel still refers to the percipients as "silent contactees." The abduction phenomenon didn't really penetrate my consciousness until the appearance of Whitley Strieber's *Communion* in 1986.

Page 185: Can you clone someone from blood? Red corpuscles have no nuclei.

Page 191: Hypnotized by a hydraulic engineer: Maybe Hickson and Parker should have been hypnotized by an amateur magician/writer for men's magazines.

Referring to people by their jobs or professions, presumably to make them look like fish-out-of-water, is one of my pet peeves, and Keel does it frequently. I have worked at many positions in my life, few of which I liked, and none of which I want to be identified with. I am not my job.

Page 193+: Thomas Monteleone: The Monteleone hoax has been documented in Karl T. Pflock's "Anatomy of a UFO Hoax" (*Fate* magazine V. 33, No. 11, November 1980); Mark Opsasnick's "The Monteleone Contactee Case and the Route 40 Abduction Corridor" (*Strange Magazine* no. 15, Spring 1995); Jerome Clark's *The UFO Encyclopedia* (under the heading "Derenberger Contact Claims"); and Monteleone's own "Last Word: The Gullibility Factor" (*Omni*, No. 1, May 1979).

Page 196: "psychology major": Keel should have stuck with thought #2.

"Some of the details": Monteleone claims he put more and more absurd details into his story, expecting to be found out at any time. His absurdities included "Vadig" appearing in public, wearing ordinary terrestrial clothing, and riding around in a big black Buick that looked and even smelled new. He couldn't have pushed Keel's buttons better if he tried.

"Even Woody was surprised": No doubt.

CHAPTER FIFTEEN

Page 206: We sure have dragged our carcasses a long way from big birds and pterodactyls, haven't we? If I had to pick and choose, I'd say that Jaye P. Paro's encounters might have been real (since she was an investigator rather than a contactee), but the misadventures of "Jane" and her ilk were hallucinatory. Jane's blank disk doesn't strike me as proof of anything.

Page 208: I could swear I saw Princess Moon Owl on Tom Snyder's *Tomorrow Show* once. Sometime in the mid-1970s Snyder dug up old tapes that had proven just too weird for his actual program, and one sequence had him interviewing a strangely-dressed black woman who hardly said anything comprehensible. Snyder explained that the woman just wandered in off the street, and the crew thought she might be amusing to interview.

Page 214: Predicted plane crashes: Depicted in the Mothman movie.

CHAPTER SIXTEEN

Page 219: energy outside our space-time continuum: A clue to Keel's thoughts? As he says, he had to be careful entertaining theories, since the phenomena seemed to shift to fit them.

Page 220: So a UFO contact might be real, even if there was no physical ship or alien, and all evidence and artifacts are created by "programmed" contactees. A bit much to accept—though the entities now sound almost like computer viruses that propagate through human minds rather than computers. We can dig an intriguing concept out of this scenario, at least.

CHAPTER SEVENTEEN

Page 232: Electronic lunacy: John Keel had no monopoly on bizarre phone calls. In their book *Phone Calls from the Dead*, parapsychologists D. Scott Rogo and Raymond Bayless describe how they sort-of discovered a phenomenon of a rare breed. Researching more than a hundred books about psychic phenomena, "we could find only four or five which even mentioned phone call cases." (Rogo and Bayless, p. 10)

The authors put out feelers for similar cases and finally found enough to fill their small volume. Many of these stories are scary and disturbing, with not only dead people's voices right in your ear, but "winds," "whistles," other nasty-sounding voices coming from someone or something else, and pathetic pleas like "I don't know where I am."

Rogo and Bayless felt obligated to learn a bit about how telephones work (at least the old-fashioned non-cell type). Whereupon they realized that, while some of the calls came from elsewhere on the line, others had to originate in the phone itself, right next to you.

Even worse, the Phenomenon came home, and someone or something started answering calls in Rogo's house when he wasn't there. Freaky enough, but Rogo writes that "burglars do not usually answer phone calls made to the houses they are robbing." (Rogo and Bayless, p. 132) If you know the circumstances surrounding Rogo's death, that line is particularly creepy. [See "The Odyssey of a Psychical Investigator: Seeking D. Scott Rogo," *The Anomalist* online, a reprint of a 2006 article on Rogo's murder. "Rogo was last seen alive on August 14, 1990. He was found stabbed to death in his home by police on August 16." —*Wikipedia*.]

Rogo and Bayless eventually realized that weird phone calls didn't stick with the dead. Eventually "we actively encouraged people to tell us about *any* unusual phone calls they had received." (p. 131) That hearkens back to Keel asking UFO/monster witnesses about any strange calls. The two parapsychologists had to admit they could not prove the voice-entities were spirits of the dead; they could be something like Keel's ultraterrestrials.

Closer to ol' Red Eyes, in 1978 journalist Rick Moran and a small group of investigators visited Point Pleasant to check the accuracy of *The Mothman Prophecies*. According to Moran, they were surprised that the people of the town—including the law enforcement officials—stood by the Mothman and MIB witnesses. No one had changed or embellished his or her story after the passage of 12 years: "not one witness swerved from their original account. Statistically, this had to be some sort of record." (Moran, p. 30)

The strangeness began after Moran and his companions returned to New York. Moran's children complained that they heard clicks and whirs on the home phones, as well as unknown persons discussing the family. A friend of Moran's claimed that she had called the house and conversed for 10 minutes with someone who sounded like the journalist and who knew things only a member of the immediate family would know. Suddenly the voice on the phone laughed "demonically" and continued, "Oh, you wanted to talk to Rick. Sorry, I'm all alone with the children." (Moran, p. 32) The next day someone called Moran's wife and warned that Moran should forget about UFOs and Point Pleasant if he cared about his family. Worried by the earlier calls, the Morans had installed a device that could trace calls. When a representative of the phone company read the trace, however, he reported, as in any good urban legend, that the call had originated within the Morans' house!

Nothing untoward happened to the Moran family. In a masterpiece of understatement, Rick Moran concludes that "The experience was, however, an eye-opener." (Moran, p. 32)

Just so it isn't all frightening, Fortean writer Brad Steiger sees Men-in-Black more as tricksters than evil alien or government agents. Perhaps that explains why his phone interferences are almost comical: "Once while speaking to a fellow researcher on the telephone, our conversation was interrupted by a metallic-sounding voice chanting: 'Ho, ho, UFO!'" (Steiger, p. 204)

Page 236: Stopwatch: Another scene depicted in the Mothman movie.

Page 237: "They" hate the space program: Perhaps Mr. Apol and his cronies realized our astronauts and probes would reveal no hidden cities on Venus or the far side of the moon.

Naval installation: In the 1991 IllumiNet edition of *The Mothman Prophecies*, Keel claims that the installation was storing nuclear waste.

Page 240: Gray Barker/Baker: I'm not the first to suggest that the strangely-acting Gray Barker was the genuine article, playing a joke on the oh-so-serious Keel.

CHAPTER EIGHTEEN

Page 245: Christmas packages: This became the seminal image in *The Mothman Prophecies* film.

Page 247: Dan Drasin: In the movie, it is the John Klein (John Keel) character who can't take it anymore and tosses out all his research.

Page 252: "Hi, this is John Keel." At last, a mere mortal gets one telling (and funny) blow in on "them."

Page 254: Strange phenomena were still going on near Point Pleasant in 1968, so apparently the fall of the Silver Bridge wasn't "the end."

CHAPTER NINETEEN

Page 258: Traffic backing up: In his interview with Doug Skinner, *et al.*, in the *Fortean Times*, Keel finds the circumstances behind the bridge collapse to be very suspicious: "The stoplights froze at either end of the bridge—they were stuck at red—so the traffic piled up in the middle of the bridge." (Skinner, p. 34)

Page 259: Electric cables parting: One witness erroneously reported the sparks as a UFO. In his book on Mothman, Donnie Sergent, Jr. mentions: "I received an e-mail from the last tractor-trailer driver across the bridge before it fell. He told me that he saw the Mothman fly around the front of his truck." (Sergent and Wamsley, p. 25)

Marcella Bennett's uncle Robert, just before he died (*circa* 2001), admitted that he saw "a man that looked like a bird" fly over the Silver Bridge just before it collapsed. (Wamsley, p. 77)

Page 263: Bridge victims: *Mothman and Other Curious Encounters* lists 46 dead, including two women who were never seen again (Kathy Byus and Maxine Turner, both of Point Pleasant).

Page 264: Men climbing on the bridge: Conspiracy writer Jim Keith sees more human than UT or MIB activity in the Point Pleasant story: "Although in print John Keel has remained mum about the most sinister of possibilities regarding the Silver Bridge disaster, he stated the following to me in a 1996 interview: "'First of all, FBI men stand out like a sore thumb. They dress the same way, they wear neckties, they wear low cut shoes, they are not the kind of guys you see in Point Pleasant,

West Virginia, on the street. They suddenly turned up just before the bridge went down.'" [Keith, p. 141]

Bridge collapse due to metal fatigue: In the Skinner interview, Keel says: "I did a study of suspension bridges, and I couldn't see how this could happen. The whole purpose of a suspension bridge is to prevent this from happening." [Skinner, p. 34]

A more mundane explanation is that an eyebar snapped—due to a flaw in it since the day it was forged in 1926—resulting in a chain reaction of snapping links.

Page 267: "Universal mind": A lot of readers have scoured the books of Charles Fort looking for this quote. It actually comes from Damon Knight's biography, *Charles Fort: Prophet of the Unexplained*: "Is there a polarity of madness, and do certain kinds of irrational states attract irrational happenings, not related to them except in being irrational?

"If there is a universal mind, must it be sane?" [p. 156]

BIBLIOGRAPHY

Barker, Gray. *Silver Bridge* (Clarksburg, WV: Saucerian Books, 1970).

Bergier, Jacques, et. al. *Extraterrestrial Intervention: The Evidence* (New York: New American Library, 1975).

Brandon, Jim. *Weird America* (New York: E. P. Dutton, 1978).

Busby, Michael. *Solving the 1897 Airship Mystery* (Gretna, LA: Pelican Publishing Co, 2004).

Clark, Jerome. *UFO Encyclopedia 2nd Edition: The Phenomenon from the Beginning* (Detroit, MI: Omnigraphics, Inc., 1998).

Clark, Jerome, and Loren Coleman. "Winged Weirdies," *Fate* Vol. 25, No. 3 (March 1972), pp. 80–89.

Cohen, Daniel. *Great Airship Mystery* (New York: Dodd, Mead and Co., 1981).

Voodoo, Devils, and the New Invisible World (New York: Dodd, Mead, and Co., 1972).

Coleman, Loren. *Mothman and Other Curious Encounters* (New York: Paraview Press, 2002).

Costello, Peter. *The Magic Zoo* (New York: St. Martin's Press, 1979).

David-Neel, Alexandria. *Magic and Mystery in Tibet* (New York, NY: Penguin Books, 1978 [1929]).

Eberhart, George M. *Geo-Bibliography of Anomalies* (Westport, CT: Greenwood Press, 1980).

Fort, Charles H. *Complete Books of Charles Fort* (New York: Dover Books, 1974 [1941]).

Fuller, John G. *Incident at Exeter* (New York: Berkeley Medallion Books, 1968 [1965]).

Gerhard, Ken, and Nick Redfern. *Monsters of Texas* (CRZ Press: Bideford, North Devon, UK, 2010).

Holiday, F. W. *Creatures from the Inner Sphere* [alternate title: *The Dragon and the Disc*] (New York: Popular Library, 1973).

Keel, John A. "Beyond the Known," in *Fate* Vol. 44, No. 3 (March 1991), pp. 19–28.

— "Beyond the Known: The Mysterious Shed," in *Fate* Vol. 48, No. 12, (December 1995), pp. 26–27.
— "Mothman Again," in *Fate* Vol. 55, No. 3 (April 2002), pp. 6–7.
— *The Mothman Prophecies* (New York, NY: TOR, 2001 [1975]).

— *The Mothman Prophecies* (Lilburn, GA: IllumiNet Press, 1991).

— "The Mutilated Horse" [letter], *Fortean Times* No. 40 (Summer 1983), p. 3.

— "Mysterious Voices from Outer Space," *Saga's UFO Report* Vol. 2, No. 5 (Winter 1975), pp. 36–38, 74–76.

— *Our Haunted Planet* (Greenwich, CT: Fawcett, 1971).

— *Strange Creatures from Time and Space* (Greenwich, CT: Fawcett, 1970).

— *UFOs: Operation Trojan Horse* (New York: G. P. Putman's Sons, 1970, reprinted by Anomalist Books, 2013).

Keith, Jim. *Casebook on the Men in Black* (Lilburn, GA: IllumiNet Press, 1997).

Knight, Damon. *Charles Fort: Prophet of the Unexplained* (Garden City, NY: Doubleday, 1970).

McCloy, James F., and Ray Miller, Jr. *Jersey Devil* (Wallingford, PA: Middle Atlantic Press, 1976).

Mooney, James. *Myths of the Cherokee* (Nashville: Charles and Randy Elder, 1982 [originally published in the *19th Annual Reports of the Bureau of American Ethnology*, 1900]).

Moran, Rick, "Point Pleasant Revisited," in *Fortean Times* No. 156 (April 2002), pp. 29–32.

Moseley, James W., and Karl T. Pflock. *Shockingly Close to the Truth!: Confessions of a Grave-Robbing Ufologist* (Amherst, NY: Prometheus Books, 2002).

Pogue, William R. *How Do You Go to the Bathroom in Space?* (New York: TOR, 1991).

Randles, Jenny. *Truth Behind Men in Black* (New York: St. Martin's Press, 1997).

Rickard, Bob. "A Reprise for 'Living Wonders,'" *Fortean Times* No. 40 (Summer 1983), pp. 4–15.

Rogo, D. Scott, and Raymond Bayless. *Phone Calls from the Dead* (New York: Berkley Books, 1979).

Rutledge, Harley D. *Project Identification* (Englewood Cliffs, NJ: Prentiss-Hall, 1981).

Sanderson, Ivan T. *Invisible Residents* (New York: Thomas Y. Crowell, 1970).

Sergent, Donnie, Jr., and Jeff Wamsley. *Mothman: The Facts Behind the Legend* (Point Pleasant, WV: Mothman Lives Publishing, 2002).

Skinner, Doug, et. al. "Lunch with Keel," *Fortean Times* No. 156 (April 2002), pp. 34–35.

Steiger, Brad. *Mysteries of Time and Space* (New York: Dell, 1974).

Stonehill, Paul. "Return of the Flying Man," *Fate* Vol. 45, No. 11 (November 1992), pp. 48–53.

Story, Ronald D., editor. *Encyclopedia of Extraterrestrial Encounters* (New York: New American Library, 2001).

Turbak, Gary. "Missing: 100,000 Children a Year," *Reader's Digest*, Vol. 121 No. 723, July 1982), pp. 60–64.

Vallee, Jacques. *Passport to Magonia* (Chicago: Henry Regnery Co., 1969).

Wamsley, Jeff. *Mothman: Behind the Red Eyes.* (Point Pleasant, WV: Mothman Press, 2005).

Appendix B: Mothman Death List (with associated events)

#1–#46: The Silver Bridge Victims
At 5:04 PM, on *December 15, 1967*, the Silver Bridge collapsed during rush hour. Forty-six lives were lost, and 44 bodies were recovered. These are the names of those whose bodies were recovered:

Albert A. Adler, Jr, Gallipolis, OH
J. O. Bennnett, Walnut Cove, NC
Leo Blackman, Richmond, VA
Kristye Boggs, Vinton, OH
Margaret Boggs, Vinton, OH
Hilda Byus, Point Pleasant, WV
Kimberly Byus, Point Pleasant, WV
Melvin Cantrell, Gallipolis Ferry, WV
Thomas A. Cantrell, Gallipolis, OH
Donna Jean Casey, Gallipolis, OH
Cecil Counts, Gallipolis Ferry, WV
Horace Cremeans, Route 1, Gallipolis, OH
Harold Cundiff, Winston-Salem, NC
Alonzo Luther Darst, Cheshire, OH
Alma Duff, Point Pleasant, WV
James Hawkins, Westerville, OH
Bobby L. Head, Gallipolis, OH
Forrest Raymond Higley, Bidwell, OH

Alva B. Lane, Route 1, Gallipolis, OH
Thomas "Bus" Howard Lee, Gallipolis, OH
G. H. Mabe, Jamestown, NC
Darlene Mayes, Kanauga, OH
Gerald McMannus, South Point, OH
James Richard Maxwell, Gallipolis, OH
James F. Meadows, Point Pleasant, WV
Timothy Meadows, Point Pleasant, WV
Frederick D. Miller, Gallipolis, OH
Ronnie G. Moore, Gallipolis, OH
Nora Isabelle Nibert, Gallipolis Ferry, WV
Darius E. Northup, Gallipolis Ferry, WV
James O. Pullen, Middleport, OH
Leo "Doc" Sanders, Point Pleasant, WV
Ronald Sims, Gallipolis, OH
Charles T. Smith, Bidwell, OH
Oma Mae Smith, Bidwell, OH
Maxine Sturgeon, Kanauga, OH
Denzil Taylor, Point Pleasant, WV
Glenna Mae Taylor, Point Pleasant, WV
Robert Eugene Towe, Cana, VA
Victor William Turner, Point Pleasant, WV
Marvin Wamsley, Point Pleasant, WV
Lillian Eleanor Wedge, Point Pleasant, WV
Paul D. Wedge, Point Pleasant, WV
James Alfred White, Point Pleasant, WV

The two whose bodies were never recovered are:
Kathy Byus, Point Pleasant, WV
Maxine Turner, Point Pleasant, WV

#47: Mary Hyre

The date game (or Mothman math) played a role in the next death. The first sighting (acknowledged by the media and first filed by reporter Mary Hyre) occurred when the Scarberrys and Mallettes saw Mothman on November 15, 1966, in the TNT area, Point Pleasant, West Virginia. Then exactly 13 months later, the Silver Bridge collapsed on December 15, 1967. The cause, according to the final government report, was that Eyebar #13 had snapped. Twenty-six months later (13 x 2) exactly, Mary Hyre died on *February 15, 1970*, at the age of 54, after a four-week illness. Hyre was the Point Pleasant correspondent for the Athens, Ohio, newspaper *The Messenger*, and during the 1960s' investigations, became a close friend of John A. Keel. (Her husband Scotty had died on December 1, 1968.)

1970—Two fiction books were published on events linked to the 1967 collapse of the bridge at Point Pleasant. One was a straightforward novel, *Beyond the Bridge* (NY: Harcourt, Brace & World, Inc., 1970) by Jack Matthews, about a man who had survived the disaster and began life anew. The other, a book with heavy doses of fiction and fact, was *The Silver Bridge* (Clarksburg, WV: Saucerian Books, 1970) by Gary Barker. Mothman figures in Barker's book, but not specifically in Matthews' book.

#48: Wes Wears
In 2007, an individual linked to the events of 1967 sent me a note and included clippings about her cousin, Wes Wears. Wears had received a medal for his heroic acts saving people while working on an ice boat in the Ohio River, after the 1967 collapse of the Silver Bridge. The correspondent noted that Wesley Franklin Wears of Point Pleasant suffered a heart attack after his heroics and never fully recovered. He lived only until *August 1972*, dying when he was only 42. His oldest son Thomas died in a tragic car accident in Mason County, West Virginia, shortly after his father's death. And Wes' daughter, Sheila Wears Pierce, 24, went missing on June 24, 1978 after walking to a local store from her Point Pleasant home. She was never found. Her wallet was located in the Ohio River, miles from where she was last seen, a year later. Serial killer Henry Lee Lucas confessed to her murder, knew where her tattoo was found on her body, but was not tried for that offense. Rumors circulated that Lucas even attended a Wears reunion in the area.

#49. Ivan T. Sanderson

Naturalist, cryptozoologist, and television animal celebrity Ivan Sanderson served as John A. Keel's main consultant on the natural history behind the reports of Mothman. Keel was often on the phone with Sanderson, who was a well-known writer and television's first "animal man," appearing on *The Gary Moore* in the 1950s. At the time of the Mothman sightings, Sanderson was the director of the Society for the Investigation of the Unexplained (SITU) in New Jersey. Sanderson was one of the first researchers on the scene of the Flatwoods Monster seen in West Virginia in 1952. He was more involved with the Mothman situation that is often remembered. The Scottish Sanderson, 62, died on *February 19, 1973*, of a rapidly spreading cancer, in his adopted state of New Jersey.

1974—Keel wrote in his 1975 book: "Only one subsequent report [of Mothman] is known, from Elma, New York, in October of 1974." (Of course, we know today this is no longer true.)

#50: Fred Freed

Mary Hyre and Ivan Sanderson were named in John A. Keel's book as having died before the tenth anniversary of his Mothman investigations. He also mentioned Fred Freed, who is little known today. In television histories, however, Freed's documentaries, the *NBC White Paper*, which began in 1960, are acclaimed as groundbreaking. The series was quite successful but ended with Freed's death. In September 1973, Keel and Freed began meeting regularly to discuss a White Paper that would concentrate on the Ohio Valley UFO flaps and other activity (Mothman) in the area. This documentary would never be made. On *March 31, 1974*, a maid found Freed, 53, dead in his bed, of an undetermined cause, which was later changed to "died suddenly of a heart attack."

1984—New reports of Mothman are recorded for West Virginia, including a close encounter by witnesses Brenda and James DeVore.

#51: Gray Barker

Besides John Keel, no person was as often on scene in Mason County, during 1966–1967, as West Virginian Gary Barker. Barker was a theatrical film booker and educational-materials distributor based in Clarksburg, West Virginia, who became interested in UFOs after he investigated the Flatwoods Monster in 1952. In 1956, Barker was the first person to write a book (*They Knew Too Much About Flying Saucers*, Clarksburg, WV: Saucerian Books, 1956) on the Men in Black (which Keel would later call MIBs). Barker and Keel interviewed Woodrow Derenberger, the contactee who was visited by Indrid Cold. Barker noted in *Spacecraft News #3*, in 1966, that when he was investigating Mothman near Point Pleasant, he found a note on his door with this ungrammatical message, "ABANDON YOUR RESEARCH OR YOU WILL BE REGRET. YOU HAVE BEEN WARNED." Over Labor Day, 1968, Barker held a Mothman Convention in Point Pleasant, West Virginia. This displeased Keel. Afterward Keel wrote to Barker about it on March 15, 1969, and a rift developed between them that would never heal.

Gray Barker's closest friend, UFO humorist and researcher James Moseley noted in his book, *Shockingly Close to the Truth*, that Barker died on *December 6, 1984*, "after a long series of illnesses" in a Charleston, West Virginia, hospital. The cause was somewhat mysterious and the diagnosis was always unclear. Moseley (who died at 81, on November 16, 2012) wrote that "the more or less simultaneous failure of various organs, due most probably to AIDS (though it was not diagnosed as such in those days)" killed Barker. In filmmaker Ralph Coon's documentary about Barker, *Whispers from Space*, the Clarksburg investigator is depicted as a closeted gay man. Barker was only 59 when he died.

#52: D. Scott Rogo

Parapsychologist and author D. Scott Rogo, 40, was found stabbed to death on *August 18, 1990*, after a neighbor in the 18100 block of Schoenborn Street, Northridge, California, noted that Rogo's backyard sprinklers had been on for two days.

Police arrived to discover Rogo dead on the floor. The home had not been ransacked. While most of Rogo's early work focused on parapsychology, he had also written on Mothman in *The Haunted Universe* (NY: Signet, 1977) and *Earth's Secret Inhabitants* (NY: Tempo Books, 1979), the latter book written with his friend Jerome Clark.

October 1, 1991—IllumiNet Press published the first reprint of *The Mothman Prophecies* in decades. It is this edition that screenwriter Richard Hatem "discovered" in an old book store and decided to interest someone in producing a movie from the book.

#53: Donald North
Donald I. North, a Point Pleasant native who saw Mothman in the TNT area in the 1990s, died in an automobile crash in *1997*.

Spring 1997—Struck by insomnia one night during the spring of 1997, Richard Hatem drifted into a Pasadena bookstore. He saw and grabbed a used copy of *The Mothman Prophecies* from a shelf, and soon was engaged in reading it through the night.

#54: Jim Keith
Conspiracy author Jim Keith died mysteriously at the age of 50, on *September 7, 1999*, during routine knee surgery, after falling off the stage at the annual Burning Man festival in Nevada. Jim Keith was responsible for first writing about a CIA-Men-in-Black connection to the initial Mothman events in Point Pleasant, West Virginia. He held the notion that Point Pleasant was being used as a "test tube."

#55: Gene Andrusco
Born in Ontario, Canada, on April 6, 1961, Gene Andrusco relocated to Southern California when he was young, then soon became an actor on television programs such as *Bewitched* and *Cannon*. In the mid-1980s, under the pen name Gene Eugene, he started a second career as a Christian alternative rock producer, engineer, and musician as a member of Adam Again, the

Lost Dogs, and the Swirling Eddies. It was as a musician that his life crossed paths with Mothman in the late 1990s.

The only movie Gene Andrusco ever worked on was Douglas TenNapel's elusive independent film, *Mothman* (2000). Andrusco was the music editor, and performed some of the music as a member of the Lost Dogs. The film was the first feature directed by Douglas TenNapel, produced by Mark Russell and Jay Holben, and executive produced by Martin Cohen of DreamWorks SKG. It was shot on location in Orange County, California, and Point Pleasant, West Virginia, on 35mm in 15 days throughout the month of December 1997. Jay Holben, the film's head cinematographer, would go on to do *Minority Report*; Mark Russell would produce *Minority Report*. A sneak preview of TenNapel's *Mothman* was held at San Diego Comic-Con on August 12, 1999, but, although the date of final release is listed as 2000, no one really knows whatever happened to the film, and TenNapel refused to discuss it when *The Mothman Prophecies* appeared in 2002.

Andrusco, 38, was found dead in The Green Room, his production studio in Huntington Beach, California, during the early morning of *March 30, 2000,* of a brain aneurysm or heart attack.

#56: Ron Bonds

The publisher of most of Jim Keith's books and the 1991 reprint of John Keel's *The Mothman Prophecies*, Ron Bonds of IllumiNet Press died under strange circumstances, at 48, on *April 8, 2001,* after being rushed to the hospital for food poisoning, apparently contracted at the Mexican restaurant, El Azteca, Ponce de Leon, Atlanta. (Before becoming a publisher, Bonds had been a rock promoter and producer. Intriguingly, April 8 is also associated with the date that Kurt Cobain, grunge rock star, was found dead in 1994, from suicide in Seattle.)

#57: Robin Chaney Pilkington

Marcella Bennett, an eyewitness to Mothman on November 16, 1966—the oft-noted "second sighting"—lost her daughter,

Robin Pilkington, 44, on *October 24, 2001*. Marcella Bennett's remark about Mothman's "terrible, glowing, red eyes" is a frequently quoted description. Her daughter's death would signal the start of a wave of witness-relatives' deaths during the time leading up to and during *The Mothman Prophecies* movie's 2002 release. Pilkington died after a "long illness" at Bridgton (Maine) Hospital. Born January 26, 1957, in Point Pleasant, West Virginia, to Robert and Marcella Wamsley Bennett, Robin Pilkington, graduated from nursing school, and then moved to Denmark, Maine. Robin's younger sister, Kristina (also known as Tina or Teena) was the child in Marcella's arms when Marcella had her sighting in November of 1966. Robin Pilkington is buried at the Mount Pleasant (!) Cemetery in West Denmark, Maine.

January 1, 2002—Paraview Press published *Mothman and Other Curious Encounters*.

#58: Agatha Bennett

Agatha Eileen Bennett, 93, of Point Pleasant, died on *January 12, 2002*, at the Pleasant Valley Nursing and Rehabitation Center. While her age would indicate a long and rich life, the timing of her death is noteworthy, coming just as the publicity for the new Mothman movie was beginning. Her son, Robert Bennett, who along with his wife, Marcella Bennett (the often-interviewed witness), saw Mothman on the second night at the beginning of the 1966 flap. We are uncertain if any of her brothers were named Julius. An individual named Julius Oliver Bennett perished when the Silver Bridge collapsed in 1967.

#59: Ted Demme

The up-and-coming rock video filmmaker and movie director Ted Demme (*Blow*, 2001) died suddenly on *January 13, 2002* at age 38, while playing in a celebrity charity basketball game at the private Crossroads School in Santa Monica, CA. A few years earlier, Ted Demme, then the director of *Yo! MTV Raps* became friends with Mark Pellington, one of the show's producers at the time. Mark Pellington, of course, would go on from his MTV award-winning days, to become the director of *The Mothman Prophecies* (2002). Demme's uncle is Jonathan Demme, director of *Silence of the Lambs* (1991) and *The Manchurian Candidate* (2004).

#00: John A. Keel (not yet)
On *January 14, 2002*, a story circulated via the internet that John A. Keel had just died. I quickly put the rumor to rest by calling Keel and confirming that Keel was, indeed, still alive. Keel quipped that everyone should be told, "his funeral is on Saturday and he will be wearing black." Keel noted that this had happened to him at least once before, back in 1967.

January 23, 2002—North America's FX cable channel screened the documentary, *Search for the Mothman* (David Grabias director; with John A. Keel, Loren Coleman, Marcella Bennett, Linda Scarberry, and others).

January 25, 2002—*The Mothman Prophecies* (Mark Pellington director; Richard Hatem screenplay; John A. Keel, from his book) opened across America. The music soundtrack CD is released on the same date.

#60: Charles Mallette
As the movie began screening in January 2002, the Mallettes were attending a funeral in Point Pleasant, West Virginia. Stephen Mallette, who was one of the first four witnesses to Mothman, was mourning the passing of his brother, Charlie, due to a brain tumor. Charles Putnam "Charlie" Mallette, 43 of Point Pleasant, had died Thursday, *January 22, 2002*, at his home.

#61-69: Mason County road deaths
During the last week of *January 2002*, which coincided with the movie's initial release period, there were five fatalities in and near Point Pleasant, in two crashes involving four

automobiles on January 26, and three other fatal wrecks in the next five days. For rural Mason County, the eight road deaths in six days was the most in 40 years, according to the State of West Virginia. In one major crash, two tractor-trailer rigs and a Volvo resulted in the death of truck driver Richard Clement, 61, of Mukwonga, Wisconsin.

February 15, 2002—Tor Books reprinted John Keel's 1975 *The Mothman Prophecies* in paperback.

#70: Gary Ury
On *February 15, 2002*, soon after the town was coming alive with all the Mothman promotions and attention, one of Point Pleasant's better-known Mothman eyewitnesses, Tom Ury, suddenly lost his 52-year-old brother, Gary.

#71: Ted Tannebaum
Executive Producer of *The Mothman Prophecies*, Ted Tannebaum died of cancer at the age of 68 on *March 7, 2002*, in Chicago, Illinois. He founded the Lakeshore Entertainment Group (which produced the Mothman motion picture) with partner Tom Rosenberg in the early 1990s. *The Mothman Prophecies* would be Tannebaum's last movie.

#72: Aaron Rebsamen
Aaron Stephen Rebsamen, 14, unexpectedly died by suicide on Thursday, *May 23, 2002*, in his Fort Smith, Arkansas home. He was the beloved son of the well-known cryptozoology artist, William Rebsamen, who did the cover illustration of Mothman for my 2002 book, *Mothman and Other Curious Encounters*. Under a tight deadline after the publisher rejected earlier images from another source, Bill Rebsamen created the Mothman painting overnight in one creative inspiration. Upon seeing the Rebsamen full-length, colored illustration of Mothman, witnesses such as Linda Scarberry said the drawing most closely matched what was first seen on November 15, 1966.

#00: Webber Falls Bridge collapse

While no direct link to Mothman has been made to this tragic accident, after years of no major bridge collapses in the United States, the timing seemed "spooky" to some. Details are included here, although the victims are not counted in the Mothman Death List total. Near Webbers Falls, 14 people died after a barge collided into an Interstate 40 bridge, sending cars, trucks and trailers into the Arkansas River early Sunday morning, *May 26, 2002.* The bridge crossed the McClellan-Kerr Arkansas River waterway in eastern Oklahoma. Seven women, seven men, and at least 10 vehicles were pulled from the river after one of two barges pushed by a tugboat struck a pillar, collapsing a 500 to 600-foot section of the bridge. Joe Dedmon, 62, of Conway, Arkansas, was the captain of the tugboat; he said he apparently "blacked out" minutes before the barge crashed into the bridge. Among those lost were Andrew Clements, 35, who was traveling from California to Woodbridge, Virginia; Jeanine Cawley, 48, of Lebanon, Oregon; Margaret Green, 45, of Stockdale, Texas; Gail Shanahan, 49, of Corpus Christi, Texas; Misty Johnson, 28, of Lavaca, Arkansas; James Johnson, 30, of Lavaca, Arkansas; Paul Tailele Jr., 39, of Magna, Utah; Wayne Martin, 49, of Norman, Oklahoma; Susan Martin, 49, of Norman, Oklahoma; Jerry Gillion, 58, of Spiro, Oklahoma; Patricia Gillion, 57, of Spiro, Oklahoma; David Mueggenborg, 52, of Okarche, Oklahoma; and Jean Mueggenborg, 51, also of Okarche, Oklahoma.

June 6, 2002—The Mothman Prophecies simple DVD (theatrical version only) was released in North America.

#73: Sherry Yearsley

Along eastbound I-80 at Sparks, Nevada, near the railroad tracks, the partially clad body of Sherry Marie Yearsley, 47, was found on June 21, 2002. Passengers on a passing Amtrak train spotted the body and notified authorities. Police said Yearsley was a murder victim, and her body had been dumped the previous day, *June 20, 2002.* At the time of her death, Yearsley was living with her mother in Reno. County records indicated Yearsley was issued a license in 1996 to marry Alfred Alsvary, who was incarcerated at the Northern Nevada Correctional Center in May 2002, on a 1-to-4-year sentence on drug charges. It was unclear if the two ever had married. Yearsley and author Jim Keith were partners for several years in the 1980s, and parented two daughters, Verity and Aerica. They separated around 1990 and engaged in a disruptive custody battle over their girls. Yearsley lost the custody case when Judge Mills Lane (later to become famous due to his court television show), discovered Yearsley had been lying to him. Today, the children live with their aunt Kathy, Jim's sister, in Oregon.

July 29, 2002—Lifetime Channel aired the first showing of the Mothman segment on *Unsolved Mysteries*.

November 15–17, 2002—Point Pleasant, West Virginia, celebrated its first annual Mothman Festival.

#74: Julia Harrison
Julia Margaret Harrison, 29, who was born on September 24, 1973, in Portland, Maine, was an associate and good friend of the members of the Portland, Oregon-based high-tech grunge band, King Black Acid. She died suddenly from the complications of an operation, on *November 17, 2002*. King Black Acid did most of the songs for disc 1 of the soundtrack CD for the movie *The Mothman Prophecies*.

#75: Susan Wilcox
On *December 8, 2002*, Susan J. "Minga" Wilcox, 53, of Columbus, died at Mt. Carmel East Hospital of an extremely rare form of brain tumor, ependymoma, which mostly strikes children under 12. Wilcox had only been diagnosed with the condition two months before. Wilcox, who saw a black "batlike" bedroom invader in her Columbus, Ohio, home in February 2001, went on to be a Mothman investigator, traveled to Point Pleasant several times in 2001 and 2002, and created a personal website entitled

"Mothman: A Life Changed Forever." She left behind a large envelope of her investigative logs for her son, Brent Fair (also a researcher on such matters), on which she had penned a note to him that read: ""B.R. Do not open until December 2002." He found the date chilling and prophetic.

2003—The Mothman Prophecies premiered on Cinemax, then on HBO, before finally being released on VHS (remember VHS?).

#76: Robert Stack
Known for his portrayal of Eliot Ness of *The Untouchables*, and as the host of *Unsolved Mysteries*, Robert Stack, 84, died at his home, on Wednesday, *May 14, 2003*. Robust and relatively healthy, his death came as a surprise to many. Stack's wife, Rosemarie, who had just returned from a charity function, found him slumped over in the couple's Los Angeles home at about 5 pm on that day. The actor had undergone radiation treatment for prostate cancer in October 2002, but his wife said he died of heart failure. *Unsolved Mysteries* was the only regularly scheduled reality program to devote a serious segment to Mothman, which they first broadcast on July 29, 2002.

May 27, 2003—The Mothman Prophecies: DVD Special Edition is released. It contains the David Grabias documentary, *Search for the Mothman.*

#00: Jessica Kaplan
This is the "death" that resulted in my creating "The Mothman Death List." What is remarkable is this person's link to *The Mothman Prophecies* movie is a mistake, an error.

Here is what I originally wrote in 2003:

"Jessica Kaplan, a crewmember on *The Mothman Prophecies*, died in the well-publicized nose-dive plane crash into LA's Fairfax neighborhood apartment building on June 6, 2003. *The Los Angeles Times* identified the pilot as Jeffrey T. Siegel, the owner of a Santa Monica construction firm. Siegel's family said that Siegel and his niece, Jessica Kaplan, 24, were flying to the family's second home in Sun Valley, Idaho. Kaplan's family described her as a screenwriter who had written for New Line Cinema. Jessica Kaplan is officially credited as one of the production crew for *The Mothman Prophecies*. As part of the Art Department working on that film about Mothman-linked disasters, Kaplan is listed as a 'scenic artist.'

"Kaplan is also known as the genius teen that sold a script to Hollywood for $150,000, when she was 17. In 2004, that script will be released as the movie *Havoc*, directed by well-known documentary filmmaker Barbara Kopple and starring Mandy Moore. The Los Angeles crash occurred on Friday 6/6/2003 (note 2 x 3 = 6, thus Friday's date can be read as 666), but then, that's probably only a coincidence."

A few years later, the actual scenic artist who worked on *The Mothman Prophecies*, also named Jessica Kaplan, wrote me and informed me that she was alive and well. The other Jessica Kaplan (both have IMDB entries), who was responsible for the film *Havoc*, had died. The "name game" had stimulated the research that led to this death list in a most bizarre fashion!

#77: Daniel Lee Carter II

Daniel Carter, 34, died on *July 15, 2003*, in Gallipolis, Ohio. Carter, born April 20, 1969, had a short but creative life, and died suddenly from a massive heart attack. He was involved with the group of artists, musicians, and photographers, all active people in the Gallipolis-Point Pleasant area who gave the Mothman investigations new life. His photographs of the old buildings of the TNT area were featured in Donnie Sergent's and Jeff Wamsley's *Mothman: The Facts Behind the Legend* (2002).

#78: Robert Sanders

On *August 26, 2003*, Robert Sanders, 44, was one of four deaths that occurred in and around Point Pleasant during the last week of August 2003, and he reportedly died by suicide. Sanders gained membership on this list because he reportedly is related to "Leo 'Doc' Sanders," who was killed when the Silver Bridge collapsed on December 15, 1967, and was perhaps a survivor, Donovan Sanders. During this unusual "death flap," the other people dying included Ricky J. Doss, 37, of Greenup, Kentucky, who drowned in a Mason County pond on August 27, 2003, and a couple who were killed in an auto accident on Highway 35, near the site of the old Silver Bridge.

#00: Daman Bridge collapse (27+ died)

Just as with the Oklahoma bridge collapse earlier, there is no direct link between Mothman and this tragic accident, but the timing of such major bridge collapses seems intriguing. On *August 28, 2003*, 27 people, including 23 school children (who were all in a mini-bus), died in the collapse of a bridge in Daman, India. Daman is about 120 miles/200 kilometers north of Mumbai (formerly Bombay), India, and is a former Portuguese colony that was liberated in 1960. The 1105-foot-long bridge suddenly collapsed when both ends crumpled inwards. Seven other individuals were missing and presumed dead. The majority of the children were from Our Lady of Fatima Convent High School. *The Mothman Prophecies* had premiered in India earlier in August 2003. The victims are not counted in the Mothman Death List total.

September 14, 2003—The Second Annual Mothman Festival was held at Point Pleasant, and an extremely large stainless-steel sculpture of a butterfly-like Mothman created by Bob Roach of New Haven was unveiled. Hayrides and tours of the TNT area were given during the early evening, after a day of local speakers and a visit from Bill Geist of *CBS News Sunday Morning*. The Geist report was then broadcast on September 28, 2003, and then repeated on August 29, 2004.

December 15, 2003—The 36th anniversary of the collapse of the Silver Bridge is acknowledged in the Gallipolis-Kanauga, Ohio, and Point Pleasant, West Virginia, area, with a remembrance in honor of the victims of the accident.

December 26, 2003—A request by the Mason County Commission to place signs at both ends of the Silver Memorial Bridge identifying it as such is "reasonable," the West Virginia Department of Transportation communicated in a letter announced on this date. The bridge has been "unofficially" known as the Silver Memorial Bridge for many years. The span was opened in 1969, less than two years after the collapse of the nearly 40-year-old Silver Bridge that previously linked downtown Point Pleasant with Kanauga, Ohio, and State Route 7.

#79: Alan Bates

British actor Sir Alan Bates, 69, died the night of *December 27, 2003*, at a hospital in London after a long battle with cancer. Bates played "Alexander Leek" in the movie *The Mothman Prophecies*. The character "Leek" was a name-game based on author-investigator John A. Keel's moniker. The activities and intellectualizations portrayed by Richard Gere's "John Klein" and Alan Bates' "Alexander Leek" in *The Mothman Prophecies* were fashioned after the real-life John A. Keel. Bates was best known for his performances on screen in films like *Women in Love* and *The Fixer*, and more recently in *The Mothman Prophecies*. Bates' very close friend John Schlesinger died July 25, 2003, at age 77, at Palm Springs, California. In 2002, Bates accepted the Philadelphia Festival of World Cinema¹s Artistic Achievement Award for Direction on behalf of John Schlesinger. Bates gained notice through appearing in Schlesinger's films, especially *A Kind of Loving*, *An Englishman Abroad*, and *Far from the Madding Crowd*. Schlesinger had also helped introduce Richard Gere to film audiences in the 1979 film *Yanks*. Bates was born on February 17, 1934, in Allestree, Derbyshire, England, UK. Bates married actress Victoria Ward in 1970. Their twin sons, Benedick and Tristan, were born in 1971. Tristan died during an asthma attack in 1990; Ward died in 1992.

December 30, 2003—A near suicide took place at Kittaning, Pennsylvania (population 4,787). In *The Mothman Prophecies*, the bridge collapse's outdoor scenes were filmed on the Kittaning Citizens Bridge. The site was used as a stand-in for the Silver Bridge at Point Pleasant, which collapsed on December 15, 1967. On the evening of December 30, 2003, Christopher Shaffer, 30, of Kittaning, while walking home, discovered a man was preparing to jump off the Kittaning Citizens Bridge into the frigid waters of the Allegheny River. After several minutes of conversation, the would-be jumper allowed Shaffer to help him back onto the bridge's walkway. Shaffer suggested they go somewhere they could talk. As they walked off the bridge at the corner of Water Street, they were met by off-duty Kittaning police chief Ed Cassesse. He happened to be at Armstrong 911 (local rescue) when several phone calls came in concerning the incident. A life saved.

#80: Betty Jane Mulligan
On *March 8, 2004*, Betty Mulligan, 82, of Pine Township, Allegheny County, Pennsylvania, an engineer, gardener, and actress, died. Her daughter, Judy Brant, also of Pine Township, noted her mother appeared as an extra in at least 15 movies, including *Lorenzo's Oil*, *The Silence of the Lambs*, and, apparently her last movie, *The Mothman Prophecies*.

July 19, 2004—The August 2004 issue of *Fortean Times* went on sale in London, with distribution to the USA, late in July. It contained the first publication of "The Mothman Death Curse" by Loren Coleman.

#81: Jennifer Barrett-Pellington
On *July 30, 2004*, Jennifer Barrett-Pellington, 42, wife of *The Mothman Prophecies* director Mark Pellington, died, in Los Angeles, and was buried at Forest Lawn Hollywood Hills. Ms. Barrett-Pellington was born December 18, 1961. *The LA Times* reported on August 3, 2004: "Costume designer Jennifer Barrett-Pellington died after an ongoing illness at age 42... Her husband included a 'Special Thanks' credit in his film *The Mothman Prophecies* to his wife for her support of him on

that film." Late in August 2004, *Variety* announced that Mark Pellington was stepping down from the job of directing the film *The Wrong Element* (which became *Firewall*, 2006, with Harrison Ford) due to the recent tragic loss of his wife.

#82: Martin Becker
On *August 13, 2004*—Martin Becker, 49, a special-effects coordinator and the co-owner of Reel Efx, an innovative North Hollywood company, died of pancreatic cancer at his Glendale, California, home. Like Jennifer Barrett-Pellington, Becker received a special "Thank You" from director Mark Pellington for his assistance during the filming of *The Mothman Prophecies*.

August 20, 2004—The Mothman Prophecies premieres on the cable network TNT. The irony, of course, is that the first "media-acknowledged" sightings of Mothman occurred in the TNT area.

August 29, 2004—The CBS News Sunday Morning re-broad-cast Bill Geist's report on the Mothman Festival from 2003, in which John A. Keel is shown in one of his rare appearances, all dressed in a white suit.

#83: Raymond H. Wamsley
On Wednesday, September 15, 2004, at 10:04 am, for some reason, I wrote to various Mothman associates and groups, asking questions about the relationship among the Wamsleys. There are two Wamsleys involved in the Silver Bridge collapse: a survivor (William Frank) and a person who died (Marvin), in two separate cars. The family name Wamsley also comes up in the witness accounts from the early Mothman days, and more recently as one of the coauthors of *Mothman: The Facts Behind the Legend*.

The next day, I wrote: "Okay, I'm beginning to build a better picture of what is going on regarding the Wamsleys and Mothman. During the famed so-called 'second sighting' of Mothman, on November 16, 1966, in which Marcella Bennett had her famous encounter, the Wamsleys were there too. Specifically, Mr. and Mrs. Raymond Wamsley were with Bennett that night."

Soon thereafter, I learned that the local papers in Gallipolis and Point Pleasant had announced that Raymond Wamsley of Henderson died on Wednesday, *September 15, 2004*. Later Donnie Moore confirmed this was the same individual who had been an eyewitness on November 16, 1966, and who had accompanied Marcella Bennett.

Later, in 2004, I would confirm through information found in various archives about the passing of Robin Chaney Pilkington, who died on October 24, 2001 (above), and that Raymond H. Wamsley was Marcella Bennett's brother.

September 18, 2004—Point Pleasant's annual Mothman Festival took place in the wake of the worst local flooding in decades, thanks to Hurricane Ivan. The annual Mothman Festival kicked off with an opening ceremony at 10 am at the Mothman Statue in Point Pleasant's Gunn Park, under sunny skies. One of the well-publicized highlights was the debut of Point Pleasant's Mothman comic book by Chad Lambert, and the Waterford, Ohio High School Marching Band performing music from *The Mothman Prophecies*. And, of course, the famed hayrides, which departed from the West Virginia State Farm Museum and toured the home of the Mothman through the TNT area. Media coverage included a local television station (Channel 13), *Animal X's* Australian crew, and independent filmmakers from Michigan and California.

December 24–30, 2004—The *LA Weekly* column, "The List 2004: Mike Davis' 6 Remarkable Ways to Die," picked my earlier version of the "Mothman Curse" as his #3.

#84: Mark E. Chorvinsky
On *July 16, 2005*, Mark Chorvinsky of Rockville, Maryland, died after his relatively quiet battle with cancer. Chorvinsky was

born in Philadelphia on March 4, 1954. A magician from the age of seven, Chorvinsky acquired an interest in mysteries and a desire to explain them. He founded and edited *Strange Magazine* from 1987 until his death. Three investigations of his overlapped with Mothman mysteries: his interest in the missing Thunderbird photograph, his debunking of the Owlman reports of Tony "Doc" Shiels, and his interviews with people who had witnessed what Chorvinsky called the "Potomac Mothman."

The "Potomac Mothman" involved a sighting on July 27, 1944, at 8:30 pm, by Father J. M. Johnson, pastor of St. John's Church in Hollywood, Maryland. Johnson, who was outside watching an approaching storm, and saw in the sky "the outspread form of a huge man with wings." Chorvinsky learned of this in January 1990, then 10 months later, in October, he interviewed actor Mike Judge (apparently *not* the actor-creator of *Beavis and Butthead*, and *King of the Hill*), a resident of Potomac, Maryland. Judge recalled that in 1968 or 1969, when Judge was eight or nine years old, a big Mothman flap took place in the area. These two cases became the foundation for Chorvinsky's "Return of the Mothman" inquiries, which we recalled anew with the release of *The Mothman Prophecies* in 2002.

Chorvinsky's death at the early age of 51 was a shock to the Fortean and cryptozoological communities, few of whom knew he was ill.

On August 10, 2005, the Travel Channel visited me at the International Cryptozoology Museum, interviewing for almost three hours for their program, *Weird Travels*. There were many questions about Mothman. At the end of the interview, as the camera crew were beginning to do B-roll taping, they asked me to raise a window. A cracked pane of glass split and sliced the palm of my hand, resulting in three hours in the hospital and stitches.

#85: Lisa McIntosh
As of September 2006, executive producer Barry Conrad and

his producer partner Lisa Petty McIntosh had been working on their documentary project about the Flatwoods Monster, Kelly Creatures, and Mothman for over five years. Their production company had completed several documentaries that have been broadcast on the Biography, A&E, Discovery, Sci-Fi, and TLC channels.

When the crew came to Portland, Maine, on April 19, 2002, they were in town to interview me about Mothman, my book on the topic, and the-then just-released Richard Gere *The Mothman Prophecies* movie. They did this, intriguingly, in a live production event in front of the University of Southern Maine documentary film class I taught. They were very professional, and it served as an educational situation on many levels.

Barry Conrad has kept in touch through the years to give me news on the progress of their project. Unfortunately, Barry's update on September 20, 2006, was shocking: "I regret to inform you that Lisa McIntosh, my girlfriend & associate producer of the documentary *Mothman: Man, Myth or Monster?*, as part of my Monsters of the UFO project, died of a rare cancer called multiple myeloma on July 25, 2006 [in Charlotte, North Carolina]. Strangely enough, she began having fainting spells while in Point Pleasant during our visit in September 2004. She was only 42 years old. Doctors said it was a textbook case, extremely unusual that this type of cancer would affect someone as young as she was. Only 1 out of approximately 200,000 people contract this disease. She will be greatly missed."

Lisa McIntosh, who died on *July 25, 2006*, had been involved with the field production of the project, setting up interviews with many eyewitnesses, connected with these cases, with the Mothman segment containing several of the original people who encountered the creature in 1966, during the McIntosh-produced filmmaking in September 2004.

#86: Bob Tracey
"Get me Cyrus Bills at the *Post*." —*The Mothman Prophecies*, 2002.

Bob Tracey of Carnegie, Pennsylvania, played the role of "Cyrus Bills," a *Washington Post* reporter in the movie *The Mothman Prophecies*. He died on *January 26, 2007*, exactly five years to the weekend that *The Mothman Prophecies* opened in theaters across the United States. Tracey, a former disc jockey, passed away from complications of pneumonia, said his wife, Marjorie Michel. Tracey, 83, was born Robert Charles Michel in Rutherford, New Jersey, in 1923. Tracey's appearance in *The Mothman Prophecies* was his last in any film.

#87: Mark A. Bennett

The Scarberrys and Mallettes saw Mothman on November 15, 1966. On November 16, Mr. and Mrs. Raymond Wamsley and Raymond's sister, Mrs. Marcella Bennett, with her baby daughter, Tina, visited friends, Mr. and Mrs. Ralph Thomas, who lived in a bungalow in a residential area near the location of the "igloos" (concrete dome-shaped dynamite storage structures erected during WWII) near the TNT plant. Marcella Bennett and the others thought they saw Mothman, and Marcella was so upset she fell on her daughter Tina. The story is well known within the Mothman literature.

Marcella told me she would never forget those red eyes. When I interviewed Marcella Bennett in 2001, I was able to meet her son Mark. He passed away at the young age of 45. His obituary in the local newspaper noted: "Mark A. Bennett, a longtime Point Pleasant resident, passed away in his home Monday, *April 16, 2007.*

#88: Tad Jones

Tad Jones of Bluefield, West Virginia, died sometime before *October 6, 2008*. Jones, a manager of an appliance store named Cross Lanes, was known for having found and cast the strange dog-like tracks in a location where the Mothman and a UFO was seen. Jones reported to Keel that he had seen a UFO there, along Route 64. In the midst of the huge "dog-like prints"— which Ivan T. Sanderson told Keel were not dog tracks—Keel and Mary Hyre found a "single footprint of what appeared to be a large, naked human foot." Was it a Bigfoot-type imprint? No images remain of any of these foot tracks.

#89: John A. Keel

The author of *The Mothman Prophecies* passed away on Friday, *July 3, 2009*. (See chapter "2. The Writer")

#90: Marcella Bennett

One of the most dignified of the early Mothman witnesses, Marcella Bennett passed away before her 70th birthday. Interviewers often felt they were talking to someone born of British nobility when Bennett would tell her story, although she was a woman of Appalachian roots. She was a grounded and refined eyewitness who was thrust into the limelight by Mothman. Marcella S. Bennett, of Gallipolis, Ohio, died Sunday, *March 1, 2009* at Holzer Medical Center in Gallipolis.

Bennett was the focus of the often-repeated Mothman incident of November 16, 1966. This is frequently called the "second sighting" of Mothman, with the Scarberry and Mallette sighting the night before being called the "first," even though today we know there were earlier encounters.

On November 16, 1966, rumors circulated that several armed local residents combed the area around the TNT plant for signs of Mothman. Then, at about 9:00 pm, Raymond Wamsley, 19, his wife, Cathy Wamsley, 18, and Marcella Bennett, 21, carrying her infant daughter, Tina (sometimes written as "Teena" by the media), along with other family members, were finished visiting the Ralph Thomas family and returning to their car. Mr. and Mrs. Ralph Thomas lived in a bungalow among the igloos (concrete dome-shaped dynamite storage structures erected during WWII) near the TNT plant. The igloos were then empty, some owned by the county, others by companies intending to use them for storage. As the Wamsleys-Bennetts were leaving, they disturbed something on the Thomas property along White Church Road.

The figure appeared behind their parked vehicle and reportedly, in some accounts, then went on the Thomases' porch and roof. "It rose up slowly from the ground. A big, gray thing.

Bigger than a man, with terrible, glowing, red eyes," reported Marcella Bennett, who screamed, and panic-stricken, dropped her baby and fell to the ground in shock. The incident is famous for the fact that when Bennett saw it, she was so startled she fell on her baby. Bennett's remark about Mothman's "terrible, glowing, red eyes" is a frequently quoted description.

As the thing unfurled its huge wings, Raymond Wamsley snatched up the child and herded the witnesses back to the safety of the house, where they were let in by Ricky Thomas, 15, and sisters Connie and Vickie. While Wamsley went to phone the police, the creature seemed to have shuffled along behind the group, coming onto the porch and peering in at them through the window. The unknown bird-like animal vanished by the time the police arrived.

Marcella Bennett was so traumatized that she eventually sought medical attention. They honestly shared their encounter with local authorities and news people, as they wished to warn others.

Eventually, the growing fame of the Mothman incidents had researchers rediscovering Marcella Bennett. As this death list testifies, in the years before her own death, Bennett was visited with tragedy after tragedy, including her son, Mark A. Bennett, 45, a longtime Point Pleasant resident, who passed away in his home on Monday, April 16, 2007.

#91: Ellie Frazetta
The wife of the man who painted the famous Mothman cover for the May 1980 issue of *High Times* magazine died in 2009. This painting would later be used on the cover of the Ron Bonds-published paperback book that fell off a shelf into the hands of the person who would recommend it be made into a movie.

Frank Frazetta (born February 9, 1928) is an American fantasy and science fiction artist, noted for work in comic books, paperback book covers, paintings, posters, record-album covers, and other media. The Point Pleasant sculpture of Mothman is based on Frazetta's moth-like representation of Mothman, even though the actual descriptions from the sightings in 1966–1967 told of an avian cryptid, the "Big Bird." Frank Frazetta also did the cover for the 1970 paperback by Keel, *Strange Creatures from Time and Space*.

Into the early months of 2009, Frazetta lived with his wife Ellie on a 67-acre estate in the Pocono Mountains at East Straudsburg, Pennsylvania. They maintained a small museum, open to the public, on the estate. Ellie Frazetta was a guide for tours there. But on *July 17, 2009*, Ellie Frazetta, 74, of Smithfield Township, passed away after a year-long battle with cancer. Her husband of 53 years, Frank Frazetta, would die within a year.

#92: Frank Frazetta

Frank Frazetta, 82, suffered a stroke on Sunday, and died on Monday afternoon, *May 10, 2010*, in Ft. Myers, Florida, reported *The New York Times*. The newspaper noted that "Frazetta was a versatile and prolific comic book artist who, in the 1940s and '50s, drew for comic strips like Al Capp's 'Lil' Abner' and comic books like 'Famous Funnies,' for which he contributed a series of covers depicting the futuristic adventurer Buck Rogers." Frazetta was perhaps best known in cryptozoology and Fortean circles for the art that would be used in a later edition of John A. Keel's book, *The Mothman Prophecies*, published by Ron Bonds. Former well-known New York City literary agent Sandra Martin told me: "John [Keel] attributed the success of that book to the cover."

Frazetta imagined Mothman differently than how the creature was described initially (which was as a giant bird, more avian that moth-like). He seems to have been overly influenced by the name, which was an Ohio copyeditor's invention that had little to do with the actual appearance of the Mothman seen in 1966–1967. But there is no doubt that once drawn, Frazetta's impact was great.

Indeed, Frazetta's Mothman cover art would then go on to influence the sculpture built in Point Pleasant, West Virginia, in honor of the Mothman lore near the present-day Mothman museum there. Earlier than his Mothman art for John Keel, was Frazetta's cover for John A. Keel's paperback book, *Strange Creatures from Time and Space* (NY: Fawcett, 1970), which has informed and influenced many Forteans from the 1970s to present. Another piece of familiar cryptid art is Frazetta's recreation of the killing of the Mokele-Mbembe by Pygmies near Lake Tele' in the Congo, circa 1960.

#93: Linda Scarberry

After a brief battle with cancer, Linda Scarberry, one of the earliest eyewitnesses to Mothman (November 15, 1966), died on Sunday morning, *March 6, 2011.* She died a Norman. As her official obituary reads, Linda S. Norman of Point Pleasant died at the age of 63, having been born on June 10, 1947. She was preceded in death by her parents and infant son Patrick.

Linda's maiden name was McDaniel. John Keel and I often discussed how her special name intersects with strangeness. The 1973 Enfield, Illinois, creature reports centered on the Illinois branch of the McDaniel family. Keel investigated a 1870s story of a McDaniel meeting the Devil in the Catskills, New York. Western Bigfoot Society member Vic McDaniel took expedition members to where he found a Sasquatch bed in August 1979. Keel wondered aloud with me about these reports, as he had returned from Point Pleasant well aware of the vortex the McDaniel family had found themselves in there.

One of the first Mothman witnesses, Linda Scarberry, was, after all, a McDaniel. Her mother saw Mothman. The McDaniel home was the focus of MIBs, telephone troubles, and poltergeist activity, thus involving Parke McDaniel and Mabel McDaniel with the Mothman flap.

Mabel McDaniel had seen Mothman on January 11, 1967, near Tiny's Restaurant in Point Pleasant; then later during March, had a run-in with one of those Mad Gasser/Springheel Jack-type fellows, the Men-In-Black. Parke McDaniel had likewise been frightened by the Men-In-Black on December 23, 1967. Keel felt the name McDaniel had a far greater recurrence in these matters than random selection.

I had found that the name *McDaniel* had a complex history in terms of its meaning. It is an altered form of Irish McDonnell "son of Donal," from an incorrect association of the Gaelic patronymic with the personal name Daniel ("God is my judge")—who, in the Bible, is eventually thrown to the lions. *McDaniel* thus is actually from the Gaelic form of Irish *Donal* (equivalent to Scottish *Donald*), and erroneously associated with the Biblical personal name Daniel. *Mc* means "son of," therefore the surname *McDaniel* is Scottish in origin and derives from the ancient celtic *domno* "world" + *val* "might," "rule."

On November 15, 1966, the world was introduced to Linda Scarberry and Steve and Mary Mallette sightings of a creature that would become known as Mothman. After parking at an old World War II munitions dump site that the locals called TNT, they saw and said they were chased by a large winged creature. They reported the incident to the police, and the sightings continued from there. The rest is cryptozoological history.

#94: Tom Campbell

News 12's anchor Tom Campbell, 68, died on Wednesday, *May 2, 2012*, after battling cancer for more than a year. Tom's first big story in a 44-year-long career was the collapse of the Silver Bridge over the Ohio River in 1967 that killed 46 people. The bridge collapse is linked in people's minds to the 13 months of Mothman sightings that directly occurred before the tragedy. The Silver Bridge fell almost exactly at the same time that President Lyndon Baines Johnson turned on the Christmas Tree lights on December 15, 1967, in front of the White House.

#95: Robert Landrum

In 2011, while I was in Point Pleasant for a taping of an interview for *Weird or What With William Shatner*, I spoke to Robert Landrum. I learned Landrum was more than the founder of The Point Gifts and Souvenirs shop. He also was an artist and had created some of the souvenirs, including a plastic model of a standing, human-like Mothman. Robert E. Landrum, 69, of Shade, Ohio, died Saturday, *June 2, 2012*, at his home.

#96: Dan Lowenski

Paul Bartholomew alerted me to the death of researcher Dan Lowenski, 62, who conducted studies on Mothman and John A. Keel. Dan passed away on *August 25, 2015*. Lowenski was a passionate, dedicated and objective researcher who served as the New York State director of the Staten Island based SBI (Scientific Bureau of Investigation). He was a former police officer and emergency management consultant who was one of their main investigators/researchers.

In October 2011, Lowenski had lectured at the Plattsburgh, New York, Paranormal Expo, presenting a talk called "Mothman: A Paranormal Archeological Expedition to Point Pleasant West Virginia and Into the Mind of John Keel." His son, Paul, did the artwork for the cover of his presentation, and constructed a life-size replica of Mothman and unveiled it there. His wife, Cathie, reported that it was donated to the Mothman Museum.

#97: Bob Roach

In terms of cryptotourism, there are only a few statues and sculptures that become meccas for people to journey and have their photographs taken in front of the artwork. Willow Creek's redwood Bigfoot is one, the Loch Ness Monster replica in a pond in Scotland is another, and the Crookston Bigfoot in Portland, Maine's International Cryptozoology Museum is another. In Point Pleasant, West Virginia, the famed Mothman statue that sits in Gunn Park in downtown Point Pleasant has become an international sensation. The statue was created by Rob Roach, one of Mason County's best-known residents and artists, who died at the age of 81, on *August 30, 2015*.

It was Charles Humphreys who had the idea for a Mothman statue back in the early 2000s. In an interview with the Point Pleasant *Daily Register*, he recalled: "I went to see Bob Roach because I knew he could make it and he'd been a buddy of mine for years. At first, he wasn't too interested in a crea-ture, but after I talked to him a little, he agreed to make it. The first two pieces he brought to me to show me were the (statue's) feet, from there on out I went to see him (as the statue progressed)."

Humphreys said a lot of research went into figuring out just what Mothman might look like, with Roach very much a part of that process and then it became about his talent taking over. "He could do about anything, especially with metal and built that with stainless steel ... it'll be here a thousand years unless someone throws it in the river and even then it'll still be here another thousand years down there."

Humphreys said when Roach was alive, he seemed "definitely surprised" by the reception his Mothman statue received around the globe. "Neither of us thought it would grow into what it is, but I knew it would make a difference in Point Pleasant. I knew people would come to see it," Humphreys said.

Roach's sculpture has become the iconic stop for tourists visiting Point Pleasant. Every day, visitors to the town are seen posing for photographs with the sculpture, regardless of sun, rain, or snow. At one point, the Mothman Museum even installed a "Mothcam" so international viewers could peek in and watch the tourists honor Roach's work. During the Mothman Festival, upwards of 8,000 to 12,000 people take their turn at the statue.

#98: James Grueser

Point Pleasant, West Virginia, police reported that James N. "Jim" Grueser, 59, of Letart, West Virginia, drowned after he willingly jumped into the Ohio River from Riverfront Park, on Saturday, *September 19, 2015*, during the 14th Annual Mothman Festival. Witnesses said Grueser seemed determined in his jump from a short height. In a behavior seen in many jumping suicidal victims, Grueser even first took his shoes off. "He jumped purposefully, there was no foul play or anything like that," Point Pleasant Fire Chief Jeremy Bryant said. "Doesn't appear as though there is any trauma or anything like that. It just looks like he jumped in." And drowned. His body took two hours to recover in 14 feet of water. Greuser's death is the first known to have happened during the Mothman Festival.

#99: Mark A. Hall

My very close friend, colleague, co-author, and fellow Midwesterner, Mark A. Hall, died on the morning of Wednesday, *September 28, 2016.* He was such a quiet force in the foundational thinking taking place in cryptozoology; it may be years before younger researchers realize what a loss this is. But for me, it was an immediate and powerful punch to the gut.

Mark's brother had passed away a few years before, and his brother's widow, Shelia, had become a lifeline for Mark in his last years. Shelia Hall was able to be with Mark on the night before he died, when he talked for over an hour to her, saying again that he was happy his research was in good hands with the International Cryptozoology Museum. Mark had been challenged by various forms of cancer for years, winning sometimes, and finally losing the battle, despite telling people he was only suffering temporary set-backs.

Mark A. Hall was intrigued by nature's anomalies for most of his life. For almost 60 years, he was actively pursuing historical records and eyewitness testimony concerning cryptozoological phenomena. Mark actively researched mystery cats, hairy hominoids, surviving anthropoids, ancient civilizations, merbeings, and hundreds of other topics.

Including Mothman. Mark A. Hall and I appeared together on *Coast to Coast A.M.* with George Noory to talk about "Mothman & Thunderbirds," on Tuesday, November 15, 2005. I presented an overview of the Mothman case, and we talked about the creature's similarities to a giant owl and may have used air turbulence from cars to facilitate its flight. Mark joined the show to share material on Thunderbirds, which reportedly have a wingspan of 18 to 20 feet—twice the size of any known birds. Hall recounted the 1977 Lawndale, Illinois, case where a young boy was picked up and carried briefly by one of the giant birds. Though unharmed, the boy's hair turned gray after the incident. Hall said there were similar instances in the 1800s.

Mark Hall then appeared alone, with Ian Punnett, on *Coast to Coast A.M.*, on June 30, 2006, on the show "Giant Owls & Thunderbirds." Hall talked about reported sightings of giant owls and other mysterious behemothic birds. Hall said American Indian legends as well as modern accounts speak about such birds, particularly in the West Virginian Appalachian Mountains. Some of these "great owls" are reportedly man-sized with 10-foot wingspans, Hall explained, and were probably the inspiration behind the Mothman stories of the 1960s. Hall coined the term "Bighoot" to describe the true origins of the Mothman sightings, which he related to giant owls. He felt he discovered they used mimicry to disguise themselves as trees while standing in the forests of Appalachia. In his 2004 book, *Thunderbirds: America's Living Legends of Giant Birds*, he dedicated a chapter to his Bighoot theory of Mothman.

#100: Carolin Harris

On the morning of *December 26, 2016*, Carolin Harris, 74, owner of Harris Steakhouse (informally called "The Mothman Diner") on Main Street, passed away. Harris was a well-known Point Pleasant, West Virginia, personality. Many tourists stopped in to her diner to talk to her and look at her collection of historical Mothman items. She also was a supporter and co-director of the Mothman Festival. Harris's father, 85, died in 2007, right before Carolin Harris's niece died in a head-on car crash.

Harris opened the Harris Steakhouse in 1969 and ran it for 48 years. The diner set in *The Mothman Prophecies* movie was modeled after Harris Steakhouse, down to the coloring and décor.

In 2017, the Mothman Museum created a new exhibit dedicated to Carolin Harris and her diner, with chairs and the soda foundation counter from the restaurant donated by her family.

The deaths of witnesses and those involved with Mothman continue. And the mystery remains.

About the Author

Loren Coleman is one of the world's leading cryptozoologists; indeed, some jokingly say he is the world's leading *living* cryptozoologist. Certainly, due to the fact he has done fieldwork, writing, and lecturing on cryptozoology since 1960, he has become one of the most often sought out spokespersons in contemporary cryptozoology, standing on the shoulders of the late great Big Three: Ivan T. Sanderson, Bernard Heuvelmans, and John A. Keel. Coleman was a Life Member of the now-defunct International Society of Cryptozoology, and is the founder/director, since 2003, of the International Cryptozoology Museum. In 2016, he cofounded the International Cryptozoology Society, and in 2017, created the Junior Cryptozoology Clubs, modeling them on the 1910-1970s' Junior Audubon Clubs.

Coleman has authored or coauthored over 40 books (including *Cryptozoology A to Z*, *The Field Guide to Bigfoot and Other Mystery Primates*, *The Field Guide to Lake Monsters and Sea Serpents*, *Mysterious America*, *Bigfoot: The True Story of Apes in America*, and *Mothman and Other Curious Encounters*). He has been the author of chapters, introductions, and otherwise contributed to more than 60 other books. He has appeared frequently on hundreds of radio and television programs, and has lectured throughout North America and Europe.

Coleman has an undergraduate degree from Southern Illinois University-Carbondale, where he majored in anthropology, minored in zoology, and did some summer work in archaeology. He received a graduate degree in psychiatric social work (MSW) from Simmons College in Boston. He was admitted to and took doctoral coursework in anthropology at Brandies University, and in sociology at the University of New Hampshire, but stopped to be a full-time father. Coleman has been an instructor, assistant/associate professor, and documentary filmmaker at six New England university settings since 1980. He was a fulltime senior research associate at the Muskie School of Public Policy, University of Southern Maine (USM). He gave one of the first credit courses on the subject of cryptozoology in 1990, and examined cryptozoology films in his popular documentary course he taught for 23 semesters at USM, until 2003.

Loren Coleman can be followed on Twitter at @CryptoLoren and on his blog, www.cryptozoonews.com. He can also be reached at the International Cryptozoology Museum, 4 Thompson's Point Road, #106, Portland, ME 04102 (www.cryptozoologymuseum.com).

COSIMO is a specialty publisher of books and publications that inspire, inform, and engage readers. Our mission is to offer unique books to niche audiences around the world.

COSIMO BOOKS publishes books and publications for innovative authors, nonprofit organizations, and businesses. **COSIMO BOOKS** specializes in bringing books back into print, publishing new books quickly and effectively, and making these publications available to readers around the world.

COSIMO CLASSICS offers a collection of distinctive titles by the great authors and thinkers throughout the ages. At **COSIMO CLASSICS** timeless works find new life as affordable books, covering a variety of subjects including: Business, Economics, History, Personal Development, Philosophy, Religion & Spirituality, and much more!

COSIMO REPORTS publishes public reports that affect your world, from global trends to the economy, and from health to geopolitics.

FOR MORE INFORMATION CONTACT US AT
INFO@COSIMOBOOKS.COM

➤ if you are a book lover interested in our
  current catalog of books

➤ if you represent a bookstore, book club, or
  anyone else interested in special discounts
  for bulk purchases

➤ if you are an author who wants to get published

➤ if you represent an organization or business seeking
  to publish books and other publications
  for your members, donors, or customers.

COSIMO BOOKS ARE ALWAYS
AVAILABLE AT ONLINE BOOKSTORES

VISIT COSIMOBOOKS.COM
BE INSPIRED, BE INFORMED

CPSIA information can be obtained
at www.ICGtesting.com
Printed in the USA
BVHW01s0304281217
503693BV00002B/171/P